PRESIDENTIAL SEAL OF APPROVAL

What a rewarding experience it has been for me and my team to help bring My Dear Boy, Jack *to life, and to tell this story. My appreciation to the author and my wonderful team for injecting their unique talents to make this beautiful book!*

Tammara Kennelly

President, FriesenPress

...concluded. I have
been very busy help
him.

Dr. ...... I am
feeling well. I enjoy
...... and I bel...
it helps me.

I am very anxious
to get over to see......
would like you......
get me over a......
...... improve......
...... being as you......
me.

I saw in the pa......
that you were......
...... and it......
me feel very good......
know you but I......
I am very intere......
...... that......
want you to......
...... of yourse......
...... there......

FASCINATING! This frail young boy, with infantile paralysis in 1935, was given the legs of a giant and the heart of a saint. My Dear Boy, Jack is Seabiscuit on two legs.

Paul Davis (Deceased)
Former Publisher of the Tuskegee News

POWERFUL! The author's portentous discovery of letters — real letters — provides for this inspirational account of Jack's growth in wisdom and in stature and in favor with God and men. Spurred by his lively curiosity and his fascination with unlikely friendships, the author has beautifully written a true story of America and one little boy dealing with polio in the 1930s.

Kathryn Tucker Windham (Deceased)
Nationally Renowned Storyteller

MIRACLES! MIRACLES! My Dear Boy, Jack could easily be several books, all working under the banner of 'Miracle.' It does not seem possible that mere fate brings together two great men of the time in their fields — Dr. George Carver and Dr. Lyman Ward. Nor is it some idle game of chance that a letter from 1936 is discovered from young Jack Harris to Carver, concerning his treatment of infantile paralysis, while the world suffers from the ravages of this dreaded disease. It does not seem by mere chance that we meet informally and learn of such notable personages of the era, as President Franklin Roosevelt, Henry Ford and Thomas Edison within the pages of this book. MIRACLES, ALL!

Virginia and Harold Hicks (Deceased)
Former Owners of The Book Shop

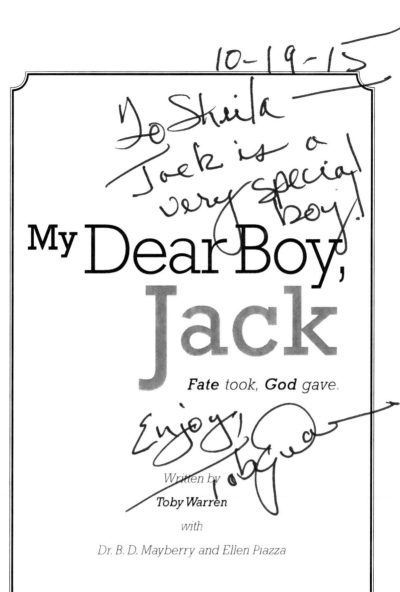

10-19-15

To Sheila
Jack is a
very special
boy!

My Dear Boy,
Jack

*Fate took, **God** gave.*

Enjoy!

Written by

Toby Warren

with

Dr. B. D. Mayberry and Ellen Piazza

Foreword by

Mark Victor Hansen

Co-founder of Chicken Soup for the Soul

Cover: George Washington Carver working on little Jack Harris' infantile paralysis in the Carver laboratory with hot peanut oil in the early 1930's, as confirmed and provided by his brother, Cullen Harris. Jack often signed many letters with – JTH.

Copyright © 2013 by Toby Warren
First Edition – December 2013

ISBN
978-1-4602-3694-9 (Hardcover)
978-1-4602-3695-6 (Softcover)
978-1-4602-3696-3 (eBook)

Produced by:

FriesenPress in partnership with Hansen House
Suite 300 – 852 Fort Street
Victoria, BC, Canada V8W 1H8

www.friesenpress.com

Distributed to the trade by The Ingram Book Company

"Jack lay in his blood after falling down the stairs once more. Two hours passed. The blood dried, and still – Jack was unable to move. He thought all was over. He had been there before as a boy, many times more. Well into his 70s in 1992, he patiently waited until enough of his strength returned... and then – pushed himself up and began to crawl – one last time..."

TABLE OF CONTENTS

DEDICATION

To Those Who Serve
Others With Disability

National Leadership Congress
Boys and Girls Clubs of America
Lyman Ward Military Academy
Disabled American Veterans
Tuskegee University

FOREWORD

Honoring Leadership
Without Fanfare

by Mark Victor Hansen

In my years of observing great leaders within their family, work and faith lives, the greatest learning experience I have benefitted from has been "leadership by example," - leaders who impact the world without fanfare.

We have available to us in every fashion, great scholars, clergy, sports figures, corporate America chief executive officers, high ranking political figures and so on – all in words and presentations by any means possible to express thoughts about the secrets to leadership.

As for me, as much as I am drawn to such experiences, every now and then, the real truth rears its head and it is then, and only then that I begin to understand what leadership is all about. I term it "leadership by example." Better yet, *"leadership for the soul."* Best yet, leadership that changes lives for the better. There are many examples of persons who actually impact other human beings to that degree. And when it happens, we see and know it. That exact moment becomes engraved on our souls forever.

This is leadership, which can be trusted, learned from and then – practiced until we get it right. Having enjoyed the privileges of being part of the *Chicken Soup for the Soul* worldwide book and program success in touching millions over the years, what lay dormant within me has been the unsatisfied hunger to address leadership in a most compelling way – with examples of leadership from peoples of all kinds, places and circumstances.

We know when a 2 x 4 hits us in the forehead. If I may suggest to any leader in place or one who is on the rise or one who has leadership as one's legacy, what lies before us is truth – leadership truth.

A non-fiction *Leadership for the Soul* series has been smartly researched for ten years, developed and now shared for all to embrace. Each volume underway shares it like it should be shared – through the soul of another who was from "no place to someplace America." With

Jack T. Harris

each work, you will stop, put it down and reflect. You will take notes and more so, you will put it into practice where and when appropriate.

Volume I, *My Dear Boy, Jack,* will deliver leadership to you on a silver platter – through a little boy crippled with infantile paralysis beginning in the 1930s.

And then, he is encouraged and encouraged and encouraged. Dr. George Carver, Dr. Lyman Ward, Henry Ford, President Franklin Roosevelt, and Thomas Edison find their way into Jack's life journey and relationships.

He is beaten up and left for dead walking the streets of Mobile, Alabama to help youth. And then, he emerges as an unequalled success story. Never would he allow his disability to define who he was and what he achieved. He was mentored by leaders and a leader he became. It is what leadership does best – for it leaves a trail of service to others to follow.

If I may suggest anything, please find a safe place where comfort is priority and lose yourself in these *actual letters* and life's journey. This, dear friends, is leadership by example, without fanfare, that will impact your soul as it has mine.

It's story time! Prepare to be inspired and challenged. Welcome to *My Dear Boy, Jack!*

THE DISCOVERY

The Story Behind the Story

by the Author

In the pursuit of understanding unique relationships in history, I made a rather bold move from 1998 to 2008. Ten years it has been.

Living in Auburn, Alabama, I decided to spend untold hours, months and years learning about and appreciating the lives of Booker T. Washington and George Washington Carver at Tuskegee University in Tuskegee, Alabama.

The university was easy to get to from Auburn, Al. – some twenty miles away. And yet, it was really hard "to get," as a personal stretching process was underway. Uncertainty was the word of the period.

There were several special moments along the way that convinced me to stay the path. The Tuskegee Archives became my second home of sorts and Cynthia Wilson, The Tuskegee Archivist, became my cheerleader, guide and resource.

I was in a world of privilege and – knew it!

At the center of this period was the friendship and encouragement of Albert Hovey and Maj. Gen. Lou Hennies, both former presidents of Lyman Ward Military Academy.

One discovery after another was first prompted by my curiosity in Lyman Ward's relationship with Booker T. Washington starting in 1898 through 1915. This led to my learning of Ward's friendship with Carver from 1898 to 1943. And this led to – you guessed it – Carver's mentoring My Dear Boy, Jack from 1936 to 1941.

The search was on! I was serious.

In the forefront of my discoveries, was meeting my new best friend and mentor, Dr. B. D. Mayberry, former Dean of Agriculture at Tuskegee University.

The process of "panning for gold" brought nuggets worthy of holding dear. I actually found a letter in the archives from my grandfather to Carver and back from

Jack T. Harris

Carver to him. Along the way, special letters to and from Carver to Lyman Ward were fascinating.

However, there was one piece of correspondence that stopped me in my tracks. While it took some time to read because of the shaky penmanship, its words had been placed on a heartfelt pedestal by the writer. They revealed the soul of a needy boy dealing with infantile paralysis, who was seeking encouragement and to be normal.

That letter was the end of many reasons that I was doing what I was doing, and it was the beginning of one reason why I felt I must see this to wherever it was leading. I had no clue where that might be. The mystery lay before me – to discover what would come my way.

I could not wait. I could not sleep. I had to know what I did not!

Dr. Mayberry and I worked together on subject of race and relationships of color, traveled and spoke together at town meetings, church gatherings, and universities, Dr. Mayberry became a friend until his death. One day, I was blessed with a note he handed me...

December 19, 2003

Dear Mr. Warren,

You didn't just walk into my life. The
Lord must have sent you. For this I
am grateful, for you have given me a
broader perspective for humanity. My
respect for others has been broadened
by our relationship, and the relationship
of all peoples, excluding any reference
to race. Our friendship is sincere and
from the heart. What I appreciate about
you most is that you are someone who
gives a damn about life and all persons
to include me --- one of another race.
Thank God for you.

Sincerely and honestly, B.D. Mayberry
PS. You brought out the other side of me!

There are no words to express what impact this had on
my journey and views of humanity.

In many respects, this pursuit I had undertaken led
to much more than satisfying a curiosity. Because of
those by whom I was surrounded and because of what
I was being challenged to better appreciate, I became
obsessed about better understanding leadership by
example. Servant leadership! Learning about leadership
on the Tuskegee campus became the secret mission of
my journey.

Jack T. Harris

It has now been ten years since I received Dr. Mayberry's eye and heart opening note. He used to ask me daily: "Where will we be when we get where we're going?" Today, I think that I can better answer his question.

From Mayberry's lips, heart and soul – and a friendship forever treasured, the National Leadership Congress was born. As we of the National Leadership Congress advance our vision to create the future through global leadership, we work daily for the causes of resilience, honor, civility and faith. For veterans, families and communities – we serve, over and over again.

As a new servant leadership institution was being established, my heart pushed me to take the letters and tell this story.

All of George Washington Carver's letters to Jack Harris began with "My dear boy, Jack."

In the name of leadership, let us share in the life's journey of a leader who arose – all starting with a letter from My Dear Boy, Jack.

The letters and the developing relationship between Carver and young Jack illustrated, encouraged, and celebrated the boy's achievements. Fifty years later, they proved to be magnets to one curious researcher; irresistible to follow as Jack grew up and moved into adulthood.

Jack stood tall in spite of his affliction. A kind of elegance – grace – showered the story in the three stages of his life shown in his own hopeful letters. His words grabbed my heart and they preserve a vivid snapshot of resilience. As Jack learned from others the value of mentoring youth and then – spent the rest of his life doing the same, his letters unravel a story that celebrates the unshakeable determination to achieve, against great odds,

Sharing the journey of Jack Harris and celebrating the millions of Americans who overcome adversity to reach their goals has given me a heightened sense of their very special places in life; these are gifts that have influenced my life's pursuits today.

You are now invited into the heart of young Jack as he embarks on a journey of hope and a record of accomplishments: some small and some sublime. Much American history will unfold as you travel this path with him and his other letters reveal just how tough life can be with a disability, though one need not be defined by it.

My dear boy, Jack would have none of that!

This story is not intended to give an account of Jack's life at every turn, but instead employs actual letters and photographs that serve to illuminate the three main periods of his life – the early years, the success years,

Jack T. Harris

and the last years. Naturally, certain questions will arise but the reader will simply have to fill in the blanks as the author has.

As I prepared this story to share with others, the discoveries made became an inclusive view - the history of our yesterdays, and a prophesy into our tomorrows.

From the shadows of disability into the light of achievement comes leadership by example - Jack T. Harris, Sr.

"The credit belongs to the man in the
arena whose face is marred by dust
and sweat and blood, who strives
again and again, who knows the great
enthusiasms, the great devotions, and
spends himself in a worthy cause."

Theodore Roosevelt

My Dear Boy, Jack

Fate took, **God** gave.

A Flashback

I

Falling and Lying In One's Own Blood: Jack's Precious Life Becomes a Flashback

"Laying at the bottom of the stairs over 2 hours bleeding, I thought all was over..." Jack Harris, September 24, 1992

It is difficult for me to envision lying in one's blood and not being able to move at all – to roll out of it. Once one has tasted one's blood, the memory never goes away! What must Jack's mind and body have been telling him? Perhaps something was speaking to him louder than words and softer than velvet. If his life seemed near its end, and his muscles had failed him, the only movement left to him would have been his mind – the place where one recounts one's life…As his heart continued to beat, perhaps he revisited turning points of his own history, in flip-chart style – the turning points that might have convinced him that he could, in fact, rise one more time, even if it meant waiting in his own blood until his strength returned. And if Jack had been into counting, it seems likely that he might have been counting his heartbeats too.

In the course of learning about Jack, I developed a strong affinity and a great affection for him. For three years I breathed the air he breathed. I walked the grounds at his boyhood school where he'd had difficulty walking—The Southern Industrial Institute in Camp Hill, Alabama — and I spent time in his beloved home city, Mobile, Alabama. I visited the house he personally built on the water, the non-profit he founded and nurtured for many years, and the cemetery where he is buried. With the vividly described image of a fall down a flight of stairs in a letter Jack wrote on September 24th, 1992, I felt his apprehension. Would he pick himself up again – stand again, after yet another fall?

"I'm still a tough old bird. I have never broken a bone falling, just cracked some. In June I messed up good. I am slowly getting back. My jaw is letting me chew and I can write a bit. Laying at bottom of stairs over 2 hours

Jack T. Harris

bleeding, I thought all was over. I'm here anyway. My best, JTH"

"I thought all was over!"

Years earlier, the 1930s loomed large to little Jack. He did not panic then, and would not now. He had been here before. The nation itself was in a panic, brought to its knees by a disease raging across the country and crippling children, adults, and even the president himself.

As his blood dried around him, he knew the taste of blood from previous falls. His breathing labored. He had to be in pain - touching his body parts to learn of broken bones, but with an unbroken spirit. Jack's head had to be spinning. In flip-chart style, his boyhood years came front and center.

Let us travel back in time with Jack, fifty-seven years - to the year 1936.

"Fall Seven Times,
Stand Up Eight."

Japanese Proverb

Jack's Early Years

II

America in a Panic:
The 1930s – A Decade of Fear

"It just was considered a feat of bravado almost to go out and mingle in public." Dr. Richard Aldrich

Polio was on the rampage in America in the 1930s. It struck indiscriminately, attacking the nerves and muscles, and at times leading to paralysis and death. Children were at especially high risk. Although there are far fewer cases of polio today, due to the vaccine, there is still no cure.

In the book A Paralyzing Fear: The Triumph Over Polio in America Dr. Richard Aldrich is interviewed about his experiences at the height of the epidemic:

"The first summer when I was home in Minnesota... We admitted 464 cases of polio just at the University Hospital, which is unbelievable. And this was a very severe paralytic form. Maybe two or three hours after a lot of these kids would come in with a stiff neck or a fever, they'd be dead. It was unbelievable. It was just loads of people that came in, sometimes with only a fever but usually a headache and a little stiffness in the neck and just absolutely terrified. At the height of the epidemic, the people in Minneapolis were so frightened that there was nobody in the restaurants. There was practically no traffic and the stores were empty. It just was considered a feat of bravado almost to go out and mingle in public."

In 1931, a Connecticut outbreak caused Wesleyan University to cancel its football season. In 1932, the Los Angeles epidemic overwhelmed the city's public health services.

In 1934, a major outbreak from May through November, in Los Angeles, drove nearly 2500 cases to the Los Angeles County General Hospital.

In 1935, Boston was slammed with a severe epidemic, and the entire city of Annapolis, Maryland was quarantined. The National Boy Scout Jamboree in Virginia was cancelled. That same year, vaccine trials of 17,000 children began, but twelve of those children contracted

Jacob T. Harris

polio and six died. In 1936, Tulsa, Oklahoma was quarantined.

In 1939, a woman gave birth in an iron lung.

Franklin Delano Roosevelt had contracted polio in 1921; he was elected president in 1932. The Warm Springs Foundation, which he sponsored, launched a nationwide crusade against polio in the '30s and in January 1938, he established the National Foundation for Infantile Paralysis.

The World Health Organization estimates that up to twenty million survivors of polio are alive today. Of the one million polio survivors in the United States, 450,000 show effects of permanent paralysis, ranging from unequal leg lengths to paralysis of breathing muscles. In 2001, 575 million children were vaccinated in ninety-four countries.

Considering that in the 1930s there was no cure and no reasonable remedy, it's no wonder that polio's careen across America incited panic. When Jonas Salk's vaccine finally overcame the virus on April 12, 1955, it was heralded as another shot heard round the world.

Until then, however, scientists built on what they knew to treat the disease. Dr. George Washington Carver was one of these.

In 1935, he received a grant to develop a combined massage and peanut oil therapy at the Tuskegee Institute in Tuskegee, Alabama. His interest in muscle healing had been longstanding.

In *The Man Who Talks With the Flowers* by Glenn Clark, Carver observes, "When I was in Ames, Iowa, I had charge of a football team and a track team. I was the official 'rubber.' Now we call them 'masseurs.' But we weren't so stylish in those days so my title was that of 'rubber.'

"I noticed then that there was something lacking in the oils used for such purposes, which set me thinking. When I came to Tuskegee, I found a healing strength in peanut oil not found in other oils. I have found great possibilities in it when properly used for rehabilitation treatment of victims of infantile paralysis."

At Tuskegee, Carver quickly earned global acclaim and recognition. In the early 1900s and for many years, few were his equal in research of the culture of whole tissues and isolated cells. Most early cells were derived from primary tissue explants; a technique that dominated and transformed cells in biomedical investigations and which has become an important staple in the development of cellular and molecular biology. This was the domain of Dr. George W. Carver.

Jack T. Harris

His intellectual gifts prompted Thomas Edison to entice Carver with $100,000 to move to New Jersey so the two could collaborate. Edison suggested, "With keys, let us unlock the universe together." Carver, who admired Edison, turned down the generous offer, opting instead to remain at Tuskegee for his entire career.

> *"With keys, let us unlock the universe together."*

Carver stayed to try to unlock one aspect of the universe alone with his microscope: the limbs of America's polio victims.

Word of Carver's treatments spread faster than Alabama kudzu in the August heat. He and his research were lavished with media attention. Despite his fame, Carver eschewed the limelight. He was far more deeply affected by the deluge of mail arriving daily at the Tuskegee post office from families asking for remedies for their polio-stricken children.

In Clark's book, Carver recounts, "On every Saturday afternoon, my infantile paralysis patients come in a steady stream from one o'clock until bed time, and I haven't a minute to myself. I hold that day and Sunday sacred for them, I invite them all to come—unless it rains."

Carver wrote in a letter dated February 7, 1935, "2,068 letters from suffering humanity are before me as I write, as nearly all are infantile paralysis patients."

At one point 6,000 pieces of correspondence awaited his reply.

The January 30, 1938 issue of *The President's Birthday Magazine* captured the urgency of the race for treatments in a retrospective of August 1937:

"It was another black August in America. Infantile paralysis struck the Midwest, the coast, the Eastern Seaboard. Swimming pools, motion picture theatres are closed. Business is at a standstill. Hospitals are crowded. Schools won't open. Police cars in the streets keep children in their homes. Doctors are all too few. Iron lungs must be shuttled about the country by airplane, by Zephyr train, by fast motorcar...this is the picture of a modern city when epidemic comes as it did last August. Cities literally bar their doors and windows to hide from this dread plague. The populace rose up, but in vain, to fight against the unseen enemy that cripples, twists, and chokes the life out of little children. The experience of the summer of 1937 forcefully brought to the public mind that fact that, although science had made great strides forward, the fight against infantile paralysis was still in its primary stages. Thinking people realized the magnitude of the emergency. Leaders in business, welfare and national affairs girded themselves for the

Jacob T. Harris

gigantic task ahead. They saw it was a fight that (required an) immediate need for a vast national organization to carry on the fight, to rush its resources and fighting men to the scene of action when epidemic struck, to find out more about the disease through tireless, heroic work of scientific men in laboratories throughout the land—in short, to prepare."

Carver was part of the far-flung band of scientists feverishly hunting for solutions; overtaxed custodians of a frightened public's hopes. The pressures and urgency of the crisis prompted Carver to explain his oppressive workload as he struggled to help young polio patients and reply to inquiries.

In a note to H.O. Abbott on January 17, 1938, he wrote:

My great friend, Mr. Abbott:

…Letters have been pouring in at the rate of about 133 per day, plus the people who come almost every hour in the day. I hope that I will be able to wade through it. Your letter is not before me, as it is swamped in the piles of letters that remain unanswered.

Very sincerely yours, G. W. Carver

Three days later, Dr. Frederick D. Patterson, President of the Tuskegee Institute, affirmed the value of Carver's research and the need to bring in reinforcements:

My dear Dr. Carver:

…On my recent visit to Pittsburgh, Cleveland, Akron, Ohio, Chicago, and Roanoke, I was asked in each city, and many times in each city, about you and the splendid work being done, and in some instances had to give a brief resume of your work. I hope I gave a fairly accurate picture, but I am sure I was unable to do justice. I am sure that as letters continue to come in as indicated in the batch of 133 received on January 6, you will need a special reader in order to save your time and energy.

Yours very truly, Frederick Patterson

Letters came from across America from physicians, families, and others seeking help. An example was a query from Dr. Frank G. Nolan, a surgeon from Hollywood, CA, who wrote to Carver on January 26, 1938, "…I have a little patient, fifteen years old, who is left with an emaciated left leg from the ravages of this

Jacb T. Harris

terrible disease, and I would appreciate some information as to the use of peanut-oil in restoring its function."

Years earlier, America might have viewed Carver's unconventional hot peanut oil treatments with skepticism, but times had changed.

In the eye of the maelstrom, inundated and preoccupied, Dr. Carver stopped time when his friend, Lyman Ward, visited with young Jack Harris in tow. Carver already knew Jack, whose polio treatments included Carver's peanut oil.

This meeting, though, may have marked the first time that the two men—one a preeminent scientist, the other the founder of The Southern Industrial Institute—realized they shared a goal: opening the door to a productive, vigorous life for Jack.

The 1930s paralyzed the nation and brought many of its children to their knees for physical reasons, while parents were on their knees for another reason. As helpless as parents were in seeking any remedy possible from any source, Jack Harris was one of the fortunate few to be treated by one who loved the young so.

With respect to need, the obvious is what Harris needed, but let us not ignore the needs of the giver.

Jack had much to achieve. He needed Carver.

Carver had much to give. He needed Jack.

Ward needed both.

Lyman Ward would prove instrumental in helping both reach their goals. During this time, Jack Harris was seeking admittance to Lyman Ward's educational institution – The Southern – where he would be a highly unlikely fit.

Jack T. Harris

"I thank God for my handicaps,
for through them, I have found
myself, my work, and my God."

Helen Keller

III

The Decision: To Admit or Not

Gaining and regaining solid footings were recurring patterns for Jack. That memorable day late in life, when he fell down the stairs and bled, was no different. He'd have to summon the fortitude to stand back up. I've often felt that he might have recalled, for motivation, other experiences where his will, grit, and self-mastery had decided his fate—in particular, September 1935.

Jack found himself sitting in the outer office of The Southern Industrial Institute in Camp Hill, Alabama. His brother, Cullen, went in first for his interview with Dr. Lyman Ward, the school's founder and president. Their mother hoped to send them to the school together. But the odds were not good.

Cullen was born in 1921 and though two years younger than Jack, was almost a foot taller. Cullen, who lived in Pittsburgh, served during his career as Chief Engineer for U.S. Steel. He recalls the day of the interviews:

"I was fourteen and Jack was sixteen. Our mother was very fond of Dr. Ward and she wanted us to go to school there. Previously, we had attended Baldwin Junior High in Montgomery, Alabama. Dr. Ward accepted me immediately, but it was a different story for Jack. Dr. Ward labored over that decision for some time. I am sure it was tough for him, given Jack's affliction. Going to The Southern would not be easy for him."

There is little known of Jack and Cullen's mother and her life and even less is known of their father.

"We were close as boys. I spent much time with him, as it seemed that other boys liked to beat Jack up because he was afflicted. I always got in the way and told them that they could not beat my brother up and I would fight for him. That is not to say that Jack did not carry his own. He did. He was a great brother. But he was disabled.

"We had a cabin on the water near Weptumpka, Alabama when we were little boys. We would swim, fish or just play in the water. On one occasion we realized that we were not alone. A water moccasin had dropped from the foliage above into the boat and started wiggling

Jack T. Harris

around. Jack took his boat paddle and began chopping at the snake. He hit the snake and it immediately wrapped itself around the paddle, which was in the boat. Jack, who could not swim, without hesitation, jumped into the water, where there were more snakes. Now I was very busy trying to rid us of the snakes and get my brother back into the boat.

"We spent time with our relatives when we were between the ages of four and six years old, but we were never wanted. We had no home. At some time in this period we were placed in the Methodist orphanage in Selma, Alabama. Iva – Mother – obtained custody through the courts when we were about six or seven years old. Then we stayed in classes together through the tenth grade. We always enjoyed each other's company.

"In many ways, we brought ourselves up, as our mother wanted us to be independent. Before 1935, I would always go with Jack to see Dr. Carver. We would hitch-hike to and from Tuskegee all the time. When there, I would wait outside until Jack came out all greased up...a little greased up boy. Jack really respected Dr. Carver and Carver was great for him. We could all see the improvement in Jack later on."

The day of his interview for admission to The Southern Industrial Institute, Jack waited patiently for Dr. Ward. All he needed was a chance. Each minute probably seemed an eternity. His small, youthful frame was rail-thin; both legs were atrophying and he walked with a limp. His right arm was drawn back and stiff. He was blind in one eye. He knew that his physical limitations would be hard for Ward to overlook, especially since every student was expected to hold a job at The Southern, to keep the farm, dairy, and facilities running.

He knew Ward was a fair man, and one who expected a great deal from his students as they earned their way through school. Every student worked hard in the classroom and on the campus. Jack was willing to work.

The wait was tough on Jack. I imagine his foot was fidgeting; it had to have been. He might have been biting a nail. He wanted to walk out before he walked in.

He wanted to walk out before he walked in.

Suddenly, he was called into Ward's office. As he was on his way in, Cullen walked out. Cullen's smile from ear to ear told Jack that his younger brother was in. Things always came more easily to Cullen.

Jack Harris's son, Jack Jr., recalls his father talking about interview day. "As my father told it, Dr. Ward did not want to admit my father. Dr. Ward was tough on my father when he went for his interview with him. So tough, in fact, that Dr. Ward basically turned my father away. But Pop would have none of that. He had to sit

Jack T. Harris

there and convince Dr. Ward to admit him to the school. My father told me that it seemed like he talked for hours and Ward just sat there and listened. When he finished, thinking that he had not accomplished his goal, he heard Ward say, 'I'll give you a chance to make it here. If you can make it here, you can make it in life.' Pop was admitted."

Cullen Harris later sent me an article—a tribute to Jack—dated 1940 and written by Lyman Ward. In it, Ward describes the interview from the moment Jack entered his office.

"He had arrived to enter school. I had expected a husky youth. Instead I saw a boy who did not have full use of his arms nor legs. He could only walk with a shuffle; his hands were just a makeshift for the hands of an average youth. He talked with difficulty. My first impulse was to refuse to accept the boy. There was something however, in his eyes that spoke to me. I believe, however, that I did tell him rather half-heartedly that I had not been advised of his affliction. There was almost no work this boy could do. The lightest work even such as sweeping seemed to get him in the 'back' as he would say. The picking of peas in the field was quite impossible for him."

Despite reasons that argued against Jack, Ward "listened" to the young man's eyes. After thirty-seven years of admitting applicants to his school, he trusted his instincts about what a youth appeared to be or not to be.

Jack and his brother could remain together and Jack had turned a corner; a door had opened. If thirty-seven years of serving as the school's president had taught Dr. Ward anything, it was to spot a worthy candidate.

When Jack walked out of Dr. Ward's office, if he could have skipped, he would have. If he could have jumped, he would have touched the top of the doorframe. If he could have whistled, he'd have done it. What he could do was what every young person can do – believe in him or herself, regardless of condition or status in life. When he left Ward's office, he was different – with a hope that would ignite a fire within, to serve him all the years of his life.

> *When he left Ward's office,*
> *he was different.*

His life was not only about to change but it would be tested in every way possible. Ward knew this; Harris would now have to earn it the hard way.

Ward was accustomed to teaching and demanding dignity and respect; he saw both personified in Jack. Still, the administrator must have labored over the decision; questioning whether the young man could carry

Jack T. Harris

his load and tackle a rigorous daily routine. Ward would not have been willing to make it easier for Jack.

No doubt Ward sensed Jack Harris's drive and quiet confidence and looked beyond what Jack couldn't do to what he could. He also saw a boy needing a place to gain his footing.

The Southern Industrial Institute was willing to anchor that boy. And it would also serve as the wind behind his sails.

"There is always one moment
in childhood when the door
opens and lets the future in."

Dr. Deepak Chopra

IV

The Southern:
An Imperfect Boy, A
Perfect School

What had Harris been admitted into?

The Southern Industrial Institute, founded in 1898 by Lyman Ward, centered on academics and existed to help each student to find his or her path after school. To reinforce the discipline necessary to thrive in life, each student also had a full-time job while attending school. Ward insisted that students work hard and reach their potential or face dismissal.

Ward was tough, but very good.

Students felt the firm resolve of Ward's leadership, and few dared to disappoint him. A boy might find himself perfecting a recitation of the "Gettysburg Address," or studying geometry in the middle of the night while running the school's printing press.

Gene Bottoms was a schoolmate of Jack Harris at The Southern. When asked about Dr. Ward's standards, he immediately launched into a recitation of "Invictus" by William Ernest Henley, without missing a word. The last verse goes:

> *It matters not how strait the gate,*
> *How charged with punishments the scroll,*
> *I am the master of my fate:*
> *I am the captain of my soul.*

Bottoms, who went on to doctoral work in geology, blurts out the poem sixty years later as if he had just learned it an hour earlier. Six decades later, he remembers both "Invictus" and Jack Harris.

Other former students recall learning much larger lessons in life from Dr. Ward, like dignity and respect. In an era that tolerated prejudice, African Americans in the South would regularly step off a sidewalk to let others pass, a practice Dr. Ward abhorred. His students were to treat all with deference. He would grab a student's arm, insist on jumping into the street to let any

Jack T. Harris

man, woman, or child pass, regardless of color, and then continue on the sidewalk.

Former student Paul Strobel recalls many such lessons taught by Dr. Ward on a watch that lasted for fifty years, from 1898 to 1948. Strobel lives now in North Carolina. His recollections reveal the impact Ward must have had on Jack, on Strobel's own progress, and on the school that admitted Jack.

As Ward noted, each student had to take on a job. Strobel remembers:

"My first job was to cut logs in the forest, matched with a laborer the school hired. It was a two-person saw and the man on the other end was over six feet and weighed in excess of 250 pounds. His arms were larger than the tree trunk we were cutting. During my first day cutting, my hands were bleeding and my body ached. It was at this time when my partner said, 'Sonny, I don't mind you riding, but please don't drag your feet as you are slowing me down.' After proving my toughness, and earning my way with many jobs, I was given the job to deliver milk every morning to the back steps of Dr. Ward's home on campus. Guess I was promoted."

"Guess I was promoted."

At The Southern, all students were required to prepare for an oral exam to be delivered in front of the entire school. When Strobel's time came, his assignment from Dr. Ward was to deliver the "Gettysburg Address" in its entirety to the school by the following week.

Strobel was required to practice in Ward's office, and Ward pushed him. If he made even a slight mistake, he'd have to start over. He spent a week reciting the address, then returning to the beginning and reciting it again. Seldom was he able to get through the text without a mistake. As the appointed day loomed though, the student felt ready. Before the entire school, he delivered a perfect speech. Strobel insisted that this experience taught him how to live the rest of his life. "When something is not right, go back until you get it right."

"Go back until you get it right."

As Strobel shared his story, I saw Harris in my mind's eye. I felt Harris reaching out toward the sun and also his searching for the moon. The sun had to have been good for the pain in his muscles and the moon for needed sleep.

After graduation, Strobel entered the Navy and spent four years serving before returning to his education at The College of William and Mary. During his first year in the Navy, he served on three different ships that went down and survived all three. On one occasion, he and other shipmates were left at sea for three nights before

Jack T. Harris

being rescued. Strobel recalls telling stories of Dr. Ward to keep his buddies awake and alert.

On one occasion at sea, his destroyer, The USS Sullivan - a 2,200 ton destroyer, 365 feet long and thirty-five feet across the beam, engaged a German submarine and disabled the vessel. The submarine surfaced and many of the German sailors jumped into the sea near the destroyer. Some of the Americans started shooting. Paul Strobel jumped into the sea, swam over to a German sailor, placed his arms around him, and swam with him back to his ship.

The captain of the USS Sullivan commended Strobel's courage to do the right thing when no one else would. There was a grace about Strobel. Sitting with him in his later years was profoundly wonderful.

Earlier, Lyman Ward had discerned that same grace under pressure when he accepted Strobel – was it not unlike Jack's grace.

In one of life's great moments, four months later, Strobel was a member of the staff at the Naval Academy Prep School in Williamsburg, Virginia. He was going through the chow line and recalls, "German prisoners of war were serving our food. One of the prisoners recognized me, got out of the serving line, and came around and hugged me. It was the sailor that I had rescued - and in very broken English, he started telling others that I was the one who rescued him.

"That was a great moment in my life."

Strobel eventually retired as executive vice president of a billion dollar company; Hydril Corporation. Among other distinctions, he served as President of the Houston, Texas Chamber of Commerce.

Not all of The Southern students were as successful as Strobel, but most left campus with a grasp of their self-worth and potential – and with a heart to over-achieve.

Jack was all about self-worth with enormous potential, if only he would NOT be defined by his disability.

Clearly, Jack Harris had gained entry into an institution where much would be expected. "Invictus" may well have captured his own aspirations: "I am the captain of my soul."

"I am the captain of my soul."

Fortunately, Dr. Lyman Ward appreciated differences and advocated self-sufficiency. He valued the former and nurtured the latter in Jack Harris.

It may be useful to share some of the philosophy of this brilliant progressive who had such a profound influence on Jack's life and the lives of thousands of young

Jack T. Harris

people—and who, in turn, may have learned a great deal from Jack over five years. The impact of Ward on Carver, on Harris, and on hundreds of students like Strobel is far greater than this story can convey. Ward was an amazing educator of the students he taught and had an insight into their souls.

Ward on … Fatigue – 1907

"I wonder how many times we look upon fatigue as a blessing. We often wish that we might never get tired. We pray always for young feet and swift and cunning fingers. No one wants to get old or to get tired. However, some of my best moments have been in the hours of fatigue. Tired out, too tired to even read and write. I have set in an easy chair and thought. And it often happens that some of my best plans come when I am too fatigued for active work. I read not infrequently of great executives who have nothing on their desks. Their whole time is taken up with thought and reflection. Details and the intricate problems rising there from are left to others to work out. This power of organization is not given to some men. Some only have time for thought in moments of fatigue. I welcome fatigue not only for the reasons herein stated, but also because I am conscious of the fact that I have been at work. So let no man pity me because I am now and then tired."

Ward on … Creature comforts and the young – 1909

"I wonder if we are not too much concerned about the creature comforts of our present day youth? We read much about special houses for the white-collar workers, easy jobs for those youth with soft hands. Will this thought and practice bring greater glory to America? I fear not. It is the pioneering spirit of old, which we need most. What is the use, for instance, of teaching the Boy Scout to build a fire without matches if they have always been provided for him, even if the government must do it, a house that is electrified? What is the use of teaching a boy to sleep on the ground if he is always to be supplied with a Beauty Rest mattress?"

Ward on… Man at his best – 1930

"Many years ago, we had a boy in school who was without money. The day before Thanksgiving, he came to see me early in the morning to know if he might be excused, in order to go to his grandmother's. I was rather displeased with the request. I had explained several times that school would continue all day Wednesday, and that there would be no going home before five o'clock that afternoon. This boy explained that he was going to walk to his grandmother's who lived twenty-five miles away. I granted his request. Later in the day, seeing the boy on the grounds, I asked him how it happened that he was still here. He then told me that a number of the students had, without his knowledge, made up a purse to buy him a ticket, so that he could remain in school during the

Jack T. Harris

day. We hear a great deal about selfishness and the baser instincts of men. I sometimes see manifestations of this but I never allow these lower evidences to sway me from the better thought that man is usually at his best, and I remember this case in particular."

Leadership, standards, compassion, and faith; just a few characteristics of one of the two men who would mentor Jack Harris. As for the other, he was a man made by his God for all of mankind.

"Education is the leading of human
souls to what is best, and making
what is best out of them."

John Ruskin

Jack's Servant
Leadership Models

V

As God Would Have It: Carver is the Man

Dr. Ward maintained an extraordinary friendship. The differences between black and white with Ward and Carver simply did not exist. There was far more common ground for them to build upon.

The friendship had begun in 1898, in the Tuskegee Institute office of Booker Washington. There, Ward met Carver for the first time. For the next forty-five years he and Dr. Carver would develop enduring bonds. They shared much in the way of educational pursuits, including agriculture. But what they really had in common was something less obvious to the eye – a mutual love for a higher power and the human condition – no matter the color.

They also collaborated for five years on one project that grew better than an Alabama sweet potato – Jack Harris.

As my forays revealed more about the bond between Ward, Carver, and Jack, I found a former student of Dr. Carver's, Dr. B. D. Mayberry. From 1933 to 1937, Mayberry studied under Carver at Tuskegee and followed in his career footsteps. Mayberry became a dear friend as we collaborated on a previous book. He knew of Carver's therapies for Jack Harris, and was able to fit the relationship into a bigger picture.

Getting to learn about Dr. Carver and his contributions was a restorative experience.

Most people know him as the horticulturalist, agriculturalist, and scientist who discovered multiple uses for the peanut. He was that and did that but he was also an unforgettable teacher, a genuine humanitarian, and a deeply spiritual man.

B.D. Mayberry majored in agriculture and pursued a career in horticulture, in the path of his mentor, and the similarity does not end there. After Dr. Mayberry earned his doctorate from Michigan State, he later followed in Carver's footsteps to become Dean of Agriculture at Tuskegee and, later, President of the Carver Research Foundation; the foundation Carver started.

Jack T. Harris

In discussing the period of the mid-1930s to 1940, Dr. Mayberry recalls:

"It was a time when Carver was becoming a globally accepted scientist and humanitarian. When I was a student, he had just discovered the use of hot peanut oil and massage therapy to help those with infantile paralysis. *Life* magazine highlighted his work in one of its first issues in 1937. He was receiving 133 letters per day from all over the world. Henry Ford was a dear friend and they spent much time together. President Franklin D. Roosevelt was a beneficiary of his work on hot peanut oil as Mrs. Roosevelt used it on her husband's legs. He soon visited Dr. Carver and Tuskegee. It was a time when all of Alabama appreciated his scholarship and his helping all people. I was very proud to be his student.

"It is hard to select one specific way in which Dr. Carver may have influenced me. In some ways, the influence was in the smallest of ways and yet was important. An example was the way he treated people that came into his life. It did not matter who you were or how unimportant you might be, Dr. Carver treated all people the same: with respect. I hoped I learned that from him. I learned my faith from Carver also. It was impossible to be in his presence and not grow to be more faithful.

"I was always impressed with how he treated the young with infantile paralysis. Students would travel great distances to receive his treatments. Tuskegee became the experimental laboratory in America for polio. One such case was Jack Harris. Carver's friend, Dr. Lyman Ward, brought Harris to Tuskegee for five years for treatments. Harris was not the only patient but I would venture to say that few spent as many years receiving his nurturing and massage treatments.

"To my knowledge, I did not meet Jack, but we could have and I might not remember it. After all, I am ninety-two. It was not unusual to see younger boys and girls come in and out of his laboratory that had infantile paralysis."

When asked about the influence Carver might have had on Harris, Dr. Mayberry thinks for a moment.

"I can only assume that he was impacted by Carver as I was. My self-worth improved. I was made to feel important and smart. There is no way that anyone could have spent five years under Dr. Carver's close watch as Harris did and not be transformed. That is what Carver did to people. Read the letters from Carver to Harris, Harris to Carver, Ward to Carver and Carver to Ward. They tell it all."

One account of his life chronicles how, when Carver was still a child, he noticed a small boy in church who was disabled. The next week he carved crutches, brought them the following Sunday to church, and presented them to the boy.

Jack T. Harris

Another account of Carver's life came from Mr. Sheridan Settler, who at the time of our visit, was 101 years old and resided in Tuskegee, Alabama. Settler shared, "I used to work for Dr. Carver and we would walk the campus frequently and talk. On one occasion, Dr. Carver witnessed a lady seeking food in the garbage and said, 'There are no germs in food from garbage when one is hungry. I have never known one to become sick from food obtained in this way.'

"He just saw life differently from most."

Carver's benevolent and paternalistic instincts evolved as he aged and reached out to people like Harris and Mayberry. About Carver's bond with students, Mayberry notes, "It was no accident that most of Dr. Carver's former students referred to him as 'father' in their correspondence to him in later years. That is the way it was for all of us.

"Carver was easy to like and to be with. To enjoy a Carver friendship made one feel more special."

Reflecting on the connections between Carver and Ward, Mayberry offers, "I am aware of the attention Carver gave to others; particularly to Dr. Lyman Ward and their friendship for forty-five years. Both were strong men with high principles. Fortunately, we have letters they sent to each other, and can learn from them today. I seriously doubt that Jack Harris would have benefited as he did for five years from both Ward and Carver, had it not been for the friendship the two men enjoyed. That friendship had to have changed Jack."

But what changed Jack? What was it that both Carver and Ward enjoyed, treasured, and spent quality time doing? They worked at their friendship and knew the rare beauty when two souls invest in another for all of the right reasons.

Jack T. Harris

"Many a man has dignified
a very lowly and humble calling
by bringing to it a master spirit,
it is the man that dignifies the calling.
Nothing that is necessary to be done
is small when a great soul does it."

Orison Swett Marden

VI

Lyman & George: Beautiful Friends

The friendship between Carver and Ward is both absorbing and remarkable, given the times and place: Alabama, 1898 to 1943.

Their rapport was powerful, heartfelt, and enduring. It lasted forty-five years, from 1898 to 1943 and ended only with Carver's death. All that time they respected, encouraged, and challenged each other. They were both spiritual men, close to God.

They were conscious of the divisions spawned by racial prejudice and refused to allow intolerance to breach their relationship. Each invested an extraordinary amount of time in the friendship and in those whose lives they improved, like Jack Harris.

Some might say that their interactions were poetry in the human expression.

Their correspondence offers an intimate look at their devotion and resolve, best circumscribed by excerpts from the more than 100 letters they exchanged. To each, words mattered. With each, words were "law."

It must be expressed that Ward and Carver each had a most powerful, spiritual side – and in their respective communications, actions, and times together – the spirit moved both to a higher plane. They fed off each other and as the standard was raised by one, the other equaled or raised the bar. There simply was no ceiling in this friendship and as you will sense, there was a goodness that came from the way they listened and learned from one another.

They shared much in common, particularly when it came to nature. On separate occasions, both men wrote of nature. Their similar sentiments are remarkable.

One is advised to move slowly through these letters, and savor the flowers along the way.

Jack T. Harris

March 31, 1939

Mr. Grover Hall, Editor

The Montgomery Advertiser

My esteemed friend, Mr. Hall:

… To me there seems to be nothing that
lifts me above the sordid and unwhole-
some things in life quite as effectively as
a visit to one of these great educational
centers of beauty and utility. A careful
study I believe will surprise and convince every lover of the rare and beautiful in nature, that we can boast of an
almost continuous panorama of beauty,
which must be seen to be appreciated.
… He who looks upon a dogwood
tree in bloom, stands at Heaven's gate,
and forever will feel kinship with The
Immaculate.

Yours very truly, G. W. Carver

April 29, 1939

My dear Dr. Carver:

… Our woods and groves have been a
bower of dogwood blossoms. We have

some wild azaleas and many tulip trees
in bloom. There is a peculiar beauty in
the tulip flower…The Judas trees have
been peculiarly emphatic this spring
with their red flowers. Please forgive this
long note and believe me always, your
sincere friend.

Yours very truly, Lyman Ward

---

*Nature for these two men was where they communed
with God. But beyond nature, the two had a great deal
to share, compare, and discuss. These letters emphasize
the friends' interactions, as later Jack Harris comes
into their relationship. If letters have ever mattered in
sharing lives, consider this to be such an example of
sharing.*

March 25, 1923

My dear Mr. Carver:

… At this moment I can think of no
man—either white or colored—who is
doing a finer thing for humanity than
you. God bless you and give you a long
day.

Yours very truly, Lyman Ward

Jack T. Harris

April 21, 1923

My esteemed friend, Mr. Ward:

… It may be of interest to you to know that a special railroad car came from Atlanta on the 6th of this month, remained at the school twenty-four hours (24) waiting for me to get ready, took me to Atlanta, and remained there until the 13th. I lived on the car during my stay there; I think this is the first time in the history of the Negro race that such has happened. I cannot help exclaim, "What has God wrought?" Throughout the entire visit, nothing but courtesies were extended. I thought you would be interested to know this. The purpose of these visits is to exploit the clays, sweet potatoes, peanuts, pecans, and other products that have been worked out here. The organization seems to be moving along nicely. Those who have given it careful study seem to feel that it will revolutionize economic conditions here in the South.

Yours most sincerely, G. W. Carver

January 15, 1925 (handwritten)

My dear Bro. Ward:

… You may be interested to know that the greater part of my work now is among white colleges, as I leave this week for N.C. where I will speak at the Univ. State College and two or three other colleges. Pray for me please that everything said and done will be for His glory. I am not interested in science or anything else that leaves God out of it.

Most sincerely yours, Geo. W. Carver

April 7, 1931

My dear Dr. Carver:

…I cannot think that in the last analysis there is much of any difference between the thing we call death and that intangible something, which we call growth. …Day unto day uttereth speech and night unto night showeth knowledge.

With best regards, Lyman Ward

Jacob T. Harris

April 9, 1931

My Esteemed friend, Dr. Ward:

I am now reveling in the strange glory
of my exquisite Amaryllis flowers, how
not quite 40 years ago I began with
two small flowers of different strains.
Scarcely four inches in diameter, one
a deep red, the other with considerable
white. How I have them from the deepest
flame color to almost pure white, I
have them wonderfully striped, spotted
and some with exquisite pencilings.
As I write, there is one before me that
measures 11 inches in diameter, a marvelous mixture of colors of the brightest
hues. I cannot but say, "What hath God
wrought." I so thoroughly agree with you
that there would be no growth, unless
there was that change which we call
death. We are too finite, my dear friend,
to understand it all.

Admiringly yours, G. W. Carver

May 25, 1931 (handwritten)

My dear Dr. Carver:

…I know of no man, white or colored, living or dead who has more finely adjusted himself to the needs of the day than George W. Carver. You have exalted by your magic touch the lowly peanut and made it chief among our foodstuffs. The sweet potato and the cowpea, you, and you alone, have placed on an eminence such as no other mental hand has succeeded in doing. All the sweets and the mysteries of the soil seem to be a privilege to your soul and to you alone. The rich colorings you have lured out of our native clay always moves me profoundly, as I walk about your work shop or studio. How is it, my dear friend that the art that died with old Rome has found a servant in your hand and heart! God give you a long day.

Yours very truly, Lyman Ward

The needs of the day... the practical and the spiritual all in one!

July 14, 1936

My dear Mr. Carver:

Jacob T. Harris

…I shall have great pleasure in using your recipe for peanut gravy. I do not know of anyone who has done so much to turn the attention of the farmers of Alabama to the peanut and sweet potato as you have. You must be a very happy man. You have combined in a remarkable way the idealism of the finest prophets with the practical everyday wisdom, which makes a man what the world calls practical. To keep one's head in the heavens and one's feet firmly planted on the ground is an endowment, which few men have. The condition of the average farmer today is serious but after all it is infinitely better than what it was when you came to Alabama years ago, equipped with youth, and wisdom, and willing hands! May God give you still, a long day.

Yours very truly, Lyman Ward

"To keep one's head in the heavens and one's feet firmly planted on the ground is an endowment, which few men have."

July 17, 1936

My great and much appreciated friend,
Principal Ward:

…Your splendid letter has just reached
me, and I have as yet not recovered from
its contents. I am so convinced, however,
that I am not worthy from any angle of
the series of fine compliments you pay
me. I have simply endeavored, in my
very imperfect way, to do my little bit
along with you and others who are doing
so much for the State and the south as
a whole from so many different angles.
My first recollection of you was at a
farmers' conference. You made a talk,
as you always did. This talk impressed
me as no other with the zeal to do
something.

…I felt it necessary to do what I could
even though the contribution was
small, and it has been a great pleasure
and indeed a privilege to work along
with you and others and make a little
contribution.

Jacb T. Harris

...So you see after all, Mr. Ward, that in writing the letter you rather put the shoes on the wrong foot, as you deserve much more credit than I, as you are in a position to render even a greater service than I. Your letter to me is priceless, knowing you as I do. With so much love and best wishes, I am,

Very truly yours, G. W. Carver

July 20, 1936

My dear Mr. Carver:

...It will surely be remarkable if out of peanut oil can come a cure for infantile paralysis. May God give you strength to carry this work forward. With all good wishes.

Yours very truly, Lyman Ward

October 1, 1936

My beloved friend, Principal Ward:

...Just as soon as you opened the laboratory door and I saw who it was, the selfishness within me of which I have super abundance sprang up and I said, "I know that he cannot be here very often, and I am just selfish enough to want to usurp every particle of his time for myself." You will never know what a joy and comfort it was to have you.

Very sincerely yours, G. W. Carver

May 4, 1939

My beloved friend, Principal Ward: (And when I say my beloved, I mean just that)

…I want to say that I am improving physically much to the astonishment of the doctors and others, as I was not supposed to come out of the hospital alive."

Most sincerely and gratefully yours, G. W. Carver

August 18, 1939

My dear Dr. Carver:

… I am more impressed with this great country of ours. And I am more impressed with the contributions, which you and others have made toward the

Jacob T. Harris

well-being and the uplift of America. I
only regret that, I, myself, have not been
able to do more in the years of my active
life. I am fully persuaded that America
and Canada could yield an asylum for all
the oppressed and distressed of the world
and yet we would not be crowded.

Very truly yours, Lyman Ward

August 21, 1939

My beloved friend, Mr. Ward:

Thank you very much for your most
wonderful letter, which reached me
yesterday. All of your letters are always
wonderful to me because I know the
spirit, which prompts them. Sorry that I
will have to write you rather disjointedly
as quite a number of people are inter-
rupting me so early this morning that
I just have to write between somebody
that asks, "Please let me see you." I am
so glad to know that you and Mrs. Ward
had such a wonderful trip. I have thought
of you both a very great deal while
you were away, and for some reason I
seem to keep in touch with you. (Mind

Telegraphy, imagine, as nothing would give me more pleasure than to have been with you and Mrs. Ward when you were seeing those marvelous manifestations of nature which the Great Creator has so marvelously opened your eyes sufficiently to see.)

…I am yet rather feeble, but I am working very hard to establish my "Museum" which will contain collections of all that I have tried to do while I have been down here.

Sincerely yours, G. W. Carver

Having walked and spending hours in the Carver museum, I see in my mind's eye Carver and my grandfather together looking over a soil sample and sharing what is possible.

October 9, 1939

My dear Dr. Carver:

…Today I note in the current news items that you are to receive on the 27th of October, the Roosevelt medal for conspicuous service this past year.

Jacob T. Harris

Accept please, my love and good wishes. Some day, I shall come to see you. Like enough, soon, like enough, late, but soon or late, you have my admiration and supreme good will.

Yours very truly, Lyman Ward

"Like enough, soon, like enough, late, but soon or late, you have my admiration and supreme good will."

October 16, 1939

My dear Dr. Carver:

…There have been some discussions in our church paper in Boston of the race question. I am not by any manner or means to be understood as thinking that the position of the Negro in the South is ideal as it is very far from it and the injustice of the Negro in the South often makes me sad beyond words. However, I feel that at the North the Negro is more

or less a toy of his White friends. Believe
me with great respect.

Yours very truly, Lyman Ward

October 20, 1939

My esteemed friend, Principal Ward:

...Sometime I feel that an open discussion of the race problem amounts to just
about as much as the discussion of war,
as we go on fighting just the same. Your
article is indeed very fine and full of
truth but many people are not willing to
try even to stand sound doctrine.

...In all thy ways acknowledge Him, and
He shall direct thy path.

...I feel that this article in part, or
entirety, can be used somewhere at some
time where it will be very effective.

With best wishes, I am Most sincerely
and gratefully yours, G. W. Carver

---

*As these letters seem to tell all, I am drawn to the
rhythm underway between the two men. The frequency
of the back and forth suggests an extreme importance*

Jack T. Harris

each placed in communicating and learning from the other. A timeless lesson it is for our 21st Century.

November 15, 1939

My beloved friend, Principal Ward:

I am so glad that you see just what I was trying to say. It does seem rather ridiculous that people cannot live in an atmosphere that is wholesome and invigorating. Your life and service to humanity lifts you so far above things of that kind that it is impossible for the person with simply a lot of free speech and no thought to understand. With much love and best wishes, I am

So sincerely yours, G. W. Carver

December 13, 1939

My dear Dr. Carver:

...I have been considerably disturbed of late with the press reports coming in about your illness.

Yours very truly, Lyman Ward

February 15, 1940

My dear Dr. Carver:

…I am sure that all your friends are deeply touched by your magnificent gift to Tuskegee. I had heard a rumor sometime ago to the effect that you were to give everything you possessed to the Institution. …No one in the circle of my acquaintance affects me more than you do…your life has been singularly free and unselfish. …May the Lord bless you and keep you for many a long day.

Yours very truly, Lyman Ward

February 19, 1940

My beloved friend, Mr. Ward:

…How happy I am to get your fine letter. I regret to state that I am yet shut in and have not been able to get to my office, which is only a few steps from my room for about five months, and naturally the doctor has prescribed complete rest. This last attack was unusually severe, but much to the astonishment of the

Jacob T. Harris

physician and the general public, I am
making a comeback and I can begin
to see myself that I am gaining a little
strength. I have been ill so very long that
it does not go as hard with me now as it
did.

Most sincerely yours, G. W. Carver

October 28, 1940

My dear Dr. Carver:

...I have long since wished that you
might exhibit your paintings. Many,
many years ago I got a glimpse of your
art when you weren't looking. I have
often smiled over the incident. Not
finding you at your laboratory, I drove
over to your room. Rapping at your
door, you swung the door wide open and
stepped outside. We talked for perhaps
five minutes and while we were talking
I had a chance to see several of your
paintings. However, I made a mistake in
calling your attention to the paintings for
as soon as I spoke of them and suggested
that you allow me to go into the room,
you politely but firmly closed the door.

So I have never really seen the products of your brush. I am glad that you are to arrange in orderly fashion the children of your dreams, which the world outside will call your paintings.

…God bless you in your labors and in your quiet hours. May your faith and strength only deepen with the coming of the years.

Yours very truly, Lyman Ward

October 31, 1941

My beloved friend, Mr. Ward:

…Had I known you were coming this way I would have made a special effort to see you, but my physical strength is yet at such a low ebb that I have to conserve every bit of it and the doctor insists upon my going in both mornings and afternoons at a certain time. I can feel my strength gradually returning. Mr. Ford has recently installed a very fine elevator for me so that I do not have to climb the steps getting to my room,

Jack T. Harris

which is of unusual value and I can feel the effects of it.

Most sincerely and gratefully yours, G. W. Carver

May 1, 1942

My dear Dr. Carver:

...You must be a very happy man in your work. The spring, I am sure, brings you an abundance of the ever recurring vistas, which have enshrined you through the days of your life.

Yours very truly, Lyman Ward

May 13, 1942

My beloved friend, Principal Ward:

This is to extend you greetings and acknowledge receipt of your beautiful letter which no one except yourself could write, as it so expresses your life and character which has followed you all the way through. I am glad you liked the little bulletin that we sent you. With every good wish, and I trust you will drop in and see us when you come this way.

Most sincerely yours, G. W. Carver

July 3, 1942

My dear Dr. Carver:

…I am greatly pleased to know that the Progressive Farmer has chosen you as the man of the year. It is a distinct honor and well placed. I know of no man either white or colored that has contributed quite so much to the lift of the farmer as George Washington Carver. It is my earnest prayer that each day may bring to you a new joy. I hope this flaming summer may find you well and happy. Serenity and courage to you for all the unconquered days that lie ahead.

With kindest regards, Lyman Ward

Carver's unconquered days ahead were few in number.

He passed away on January 5, 1943. Death, though, was part of a continuum for the agriculturist who appreciated seasons of growth, dormancy, and death. As he once wrote to Ward…

Jacob T. Harris

"There would be no growth, unless there was that change which we call death. We are too finite, my dear friend, to understand it all."

The two men had sustained their relationship since meeting in the office of Booker T. Washington forty-five years earlier. Their written exchanges demonstrate a profound depth of feeling about professional, social, and personal issues, and about each other, and they set the stage for the partnership that would nurture Jack Harris.

What we have available to us for background is an additional two men who were also stricken with infantile paralysis in the 1930s. In that Harris had died many years earlier, I had to find ways to try to understand what he felt, experienced, and became. These men knew one another, as they had attended the same high school in Montgomery, Al. Meeting them one-on-one and learning from their stories about Carver and their own lives gave me a valuable insight as to what the Carver-Harris relationship may have been like.

As the two men and I spoke of Carver and their experiences with him, my heart leapt with joy. I knew it! I knew that Harris had in some way been nurtured as they had been and that his future success could be attributed to what Carver had rubbed on the three boys' muscle tissue – not hot peanut oil, but HOPE!

"Friendship, indeed, is one of the greatest boons God can bestow on man. It is a union of our finest feelings; a disinterested binding of hearts, and sympathy between two souls. It is an indefinable trust we repose in one another, a constant communication between two minds, and an unremitting anxiety for each other's souls."

James Langdon Hill

Two Great Young Examples
of Carver's Work

VII

Been There, Done That:
Fitzpatrick and Worthington

Navigating research road, I had the great fortune to come upon two remarkable Alabama men who illuminated the era of George Washington Carver as well as the probable experiences of Jack Harris.

Tom Fitzpatrick and James Worthington were both stricken with polio when young; both were schoolmates in Montgomery, Alabama in the 1930s; and both found their way to Dr. Carver for treatment in the years that Jack did. Their memories reveal what Jack's life may have been like before, while, and after fate delivered him to the treatment table in Tuskegee.

Fitzpatrick and Worthington welcomed me and eagerly shared vignettes from their days with Carver. In separate visits with each, it became clear to me that the two men shared values, lifestyles, and deep appreciation for how Dr. Carver had altered their lives nearly seven decades ago. He had helped them walk – albeit with canes and crutches. He'd also helped quell the panic swirling around their families when the epidemic had overtaken their lives.

Tom Fitzpatrick (Now Deceased)

Let me describe the life and surroundings of Fitzpatrick, as upon my entry, I was taken with a different world – a world of scholarship, brilliance, and leadership.

Tom Fitzpatrick's den had a soothing atmosphere with a Library full of stimulating works. On one side sat his sofa, a chair, and a table, all facing a comforting fireplace with a rocking chair to its right. On the mantle rested a venerable Westminster clock he had purchased for his wife in 1957, when they were married. "I live by the Westminster," he said.

"I live by the Westminster."

This third of the room was a reader's delight. Surrounding his enormous desk were floor to ceiling books on three sides. He told me that his favorites were the six Jane Austin novels, which he has read over and

Jack T. Harris

over. His favorite was *Pride and Prejudice*, which he characterized as "human and witty."

On one wall was the Shakespeare section. Shakespeare was his passion; he had written twenty-eight articles about the bard and had never missed a Broadway production of one of Shakespeare's plays.

Tom's den was a room for relaxing, writing, reading, living - a place for this quintessential southern gentleman to gather his thoughts across eight dynamic decades.

When with him, I did not wish to talk; I just wanted to feel his space. He understood.

Fitzpatrick started his own law practice in Montgomery, Alabama and practiced alone until he retired, specializing in real estate law. He and his wife, Lillian, who died in 2003, had three children. Two graduated from Harvard and one from Columbia. His great grandfather, Ben Fitzpatrick, served as Governor of Alabama.

As hobbies, he built furniture and ship models. His most famous shipbuilding project required 2,000 hours and was modeled on the actual plans for the CSS *Alabama*, the most famous ship of the Confederacy.

I so wanted to board this ship.

Among his furniture masterpieces was a replica of the Martha Washington sewing cabinet.

Beautiful it was.

Although he used a wheelchair from ages seven to nine, crutches for sixty years, and had been back in a wheelchair since 1991, polio clearly had done nothing to diminish the man's passions, accomplishments, and drive.

Fitzpatrick confirmed:

"I haven't missed too much. Having a disability like this made me very self-sufficient very young. I attended Alabama and majored in English. Then I went to law school for three years."

Fitzpatrick was a member of Phi Beta Kappa and graduated first in his class in law school.

When Fitzpatrick's thoughts turned to Dr. George W. Carver, his eyes lowered in respect. He described Dr. Carver as "…esteemed around the world more than any Alabamian before him or since."

He began, "Infantile paralysis attacked me when I was seven. It was very painful and the first two weeks when those nerves were destroyed, I remember the agony. I could not stand a sheet over my body."

The excruciating ravages of the first years of the disease bequeathed dark moments upon polio's victims but the human mind has the capacity to dim the pain while leaving bright memories intact.

Jack T. Harris

"Before Dr. Carver worked on me, I lived at Warm Springs, Georgia for fourteen months. We lived in a cottage in 1931 and it was there that I met Franklin D. Roosevelt. He was governor at the time, about to be elected president. We were both wheelchair-bound and played water polo together. My mother sat by the pool with Eleanor Roosevelt and taught her the properties of 'grits.' Imagine at nine years old, to have played water polo with the soon-to-be-elected President of the United States.

"In 1936, at the age of thirteen, for months I was driven forty miles from Montgomery to Tuskegee, weekly, to be rubbed by Dr. Carver with peanut oil, in the hope that my polio-afflicted legs might be strengthened. My entire family went with me and the treatments were always on Sunday, when Dr. Carver had some time to see me. In one conversation with my father, he commented, 'I was sold for a racehorse.'

"I was sold for a racehorse."

"I have vivid memories of the brilliant patchwork quilt and eighteen-inch-thick feather mattress on his bed, both sewn by Dr. Carver and employed as a treatment table, and recall as well the collection of African blow-guns and poison darts mounted on his wall, which I studied every session.

"When I was being treated by Carver, he was a world celebrity. Mahatma Gandhi solicited his advice for India's agricultural system, and he declined Stalin's invitation to Russia, to supervise that nation's cotton plantations. In 1943, FDR honored Dr. Carver with the government's purchase of most of the Carver farm in order to turn the land into a national monument, the first ever dedicated to an African-American.

"With a still-clear memory of those patient massages by his knobby hands, I decided long ago that it makes no difference whether Dr. Carver was a wizard, a scientist, or a lucky fumbler. What he was to me, then and now, is epitomized on his tombstone on the campus of Tuskegee University: 'He could have added fortune to fame, but caring for neither, he found happiness and honor in being helpful to the world.'

"My family and I heard a story that was running through the campus at the time and everyone believed it to be true. It seems that an elderly white woman stopped Dr. Carver on one of his early morning walks. The woman, not knowing who he was, said, 'Uncle, I'll give you fifty cents to weed my garden.'

"Dr. Carver regarded the garden for a moment and then took off his coat and with her hoe and trowel proceeded to give it a thorough weeding. When finished, he put back on his coat, declined payment and completed his walk. Later, he was asked by someone who noticed him

Jack T. Harris

weeding the lady's garden why hadn't he told her who he was. Dr. Carver said, 'If I had, she wouldn't have let me weed her garden, and she badly needed the help.'

"That was the man who let me impose on his Sundays without a penny's pay. I will never forget Dr. Carver and his time given to me; I was one of the fortunate few to benefit from his concern and attention for my condition."

I asked Mr. Fitzpatrick if others understood and responded to the conditions and needs of the disabled.

"America has been good, but slow," he said. "I recall in law school, I had to get to the fourth floor to use the law library and had to climb forty-eight steps. I never forgot those steps. I had to go up the same way I came down: backwards. Try to climb steps backwards!"

Sixty years later, he remembered every step.

Fitzpatrick's vivid reminiscences drew me back in time, to Jack Harris. The young Jack must have seen what Fitzpatrick saw; the cheerful quilts, the exotic African memorabilia. He must have felt the same physical agony. He clearly shared the same spirit, courage, and will to succeed, although in different career pursuits. He benefited from the benevolence and brainpower of Dr. Carver—and from Carver's colorblindness and transcending of the race consciousness of the era.

As Tom Fitzpatrick concluded from the den that housed his closest keepsakes, "Dr. Carver was a man I think about most of my life. No one who ever met Carver was ever the same."

Respectfully, I must share that in leaving Mr. Fitzpatrick and his sacred space, I have never been the same since. It was from that moment that I knew what I must do – My Dear Boy, Jack must see the light of day – one day.

Perhaps, a day late in 2013 is that day.

James Worthington (Now Deceased)

What were the chances of happening upon a second alumnus of Carver's school of hope and circle of care, still residing in Montgomery, Alabama?

There he was, found on July 22, 2004: Eighty-five-year-old James Worthington, who had spent six years, 1933 to1938, tended to by Carver. Worthington's mother and aunt served as drivers to Tuskegee from his home in Montgomery. He invited me to his home for a visit, and immediately remembered Tom Fitzpatrick, who had attended the same school at the same time, although in a different grade.

"Tom used to read the Bible to the school in auditorium before gatherings. I was always impressed with him," Worthington recalls.

Jack T. Harris

Worthington had spent the past fifty-two years in the insurance business, and had recently retired. His passion and avocation; vocational counseling for the handicapped. He is a beloved presence in Montgomery, where he served as president of the Jaycees and was one of twelve charter members of Kiwanis. He and his wife, Ann, who passed away in 1990, had two children.

A more distinguished gentleman would be hard to find. He is wheelchair-bound now – or more accurately, motorized scooter-bound. His outgoing, engaging manner makes visitors feel right at home, and he invites them into his past and present with equal warmth.

A painting over the fireplace in his den commands attention. It's of a man, comfortable in his own skin, with penetrating eyes, and with poise. It's a painting of Worthington. I had to ask!

He told me that he and his wife had agreed that each would sit for a portrait for each other. She wanted him to go first and, like a smart husband, he heeded. The work was finished and then placed in their home where Ann wanted it. I had the feeling that Ann got what Ann wanted!

She died soon afterwards.

Their agreement was unfinished. Worthington called a friend and asked him if he would paint his wife from a photo he loved. Months later, the doorbell rang and there was the image of the love of his life – agreement complete…heart at peace.

Worthington opens other windows on his world with ease and confidence.

As the word "confidence" surfaces once more, I wonder. is confidence what Carver gave Fitzpatrick and did he do the same for Worthington… and Harris? I believe it to be so.

A music lover and gifted singer, he revels in his recordings, keyboard, and sheet music. In the corner of his den is a mini-music studio. This was a special seat of honor for one of his many gifts in life. Upon request he belts out a vibrant rendition of "When You're Smiling."

When you're smiling,
When you're smiling,
The whole world smiles with you!

If ever a song fit the man and his life's journey, this was it. He insists, "Laughing and singing are the best medicine in life. Music has been my life. When I really took off in life was after joining the Glee Club in high school.

I was afflicted yes, but I was also blessed twice more with my singing. Fate took, God gave."

"Fate took, God gave."

Jacob T. Harris

Fate took, God gave. Fate took, God gave. Fate took, God gave.

He said, "Life is great. I can push one button today and literally roll right into my van. Unbelievable."

The word, afflicted, – how does he feel about it? "I like that word, afflicted. Handicapped is a terrible word. Physically-challenged, is politically correct but afflicted is better.

"Handicapped suggests that all of me is disabled and believe me; all of me was never disabled. A part of me, yes, but never all of me. I think when people look at me; they assume that all of me is challenged. What really gets me is the way people look at me and turn the other way because they do not know how to deal with me. Here I am on my scooter and I can read it on their faces. Some say 'I'm sorry.' I respond with, 'Sorry for what?'

"People just do not understand persons with affliction and most do not work at trying to understand. I always feel sorry for them. It is never about me; it tells me much about them. When someone sees me as the complete human being that I am, I know all I need to know about him or her.

"We need to educate, as most people do not want to understand; that is, until someone they love is afflicted. As for the rest, first they have to choose to want to understand. Many do not care.

"Many do not care."

"I have freedom of movement today. But when I was thirteen and became afflicted, I was told that I would never walk again, by the doctors. My mother and father took me to Dr. Carver. Once there, the cadets at Tuskegee came out to the car, picked me up and took me to Carver. He knelt down in front of me and asked me to pull up my pants legs. At that first visit, after looking me over, he told me, 'You'll be playing football by your senior year.'

"I believed him. Mother started crying; she cried a lot. I have never cried from the first day. On one visit, Dr. Carver was working on me and said, 'The master said for me to tell you if you don't do what I tell you to do in your exercises, you will not walk again.' I never did not obey Dr. Carver for one day.

"I sat in his room with my parents; it was a marvelous room, with all those artifacts and bottles, and modest. From the beginning, my family wanted me in a wheel-chair, but I insisted no. When I began to walk some, I walked with a cane, not crutches. Since 1934, I have been known as the 'man with a cane.'"

Unlike Tom Fitzpatrick, Worthington had no pain associated with his polio at any point. He considers himself very fortunate in that regard and others.

Jacob T. Harris

"I am one of the most blessed people ever to live. No one has ever hurt my feelings or treated me with disrespect. If they did, I never knew it. I would not let others influence me in that way. I learned this early and directly from Dr. Carver. I know who I am and did back then.

"Adaptability was the greatest trait I learned from Carver and that was the best thing to come out of this affliction. I don't panic when things happen like many do.

"Carver had a great attitude and I think I do as well. This is what I believe: when you throw it out there, it comes back. When I could walk, I was very timid up until twelve years old. When I could not walk, I became a better person with confidence. Where do you suppose that came from in my life? Who helped me to grow in self-worth at a time when I should have been crying all the time?

"Even my family benefited from my affliction, particularly my two children. They grew up with a sense of the world differently and perhaps better than most children. Parenting for me was easier because of my condition."

As my visit with Worthington nears an end, I mention the swimming pool in the back yard. Does he swim?

"I swim every day or least regularly…good for my body. When Ann was alive, we would swim together. I would put on waltzes and direct the music through our outdoor speakers and she and I would swim to music. I could really dance in the pool."

"I could really dance in the pool."

As I drove away from Worthington's home, I reflected on one of the touching moments. Very low on the wall near his music area, next to his seat was a small-framed copy of The Lord's Prayer. I asked him about it. He took a moment and said, "I used to sing it more than hundreds of times as a boy. That is my personal copy I used in the 1930s to sing from. It is dear to me."

When he said that the song was dear to him, I saw that his passion for life and his God was truly profound. As I started to leave, I heard his soft voice singing – Our Father, who art in Heaven..."

Have you ever walked away from someone where you instantly felt like a better person because of being in their company? I have!

Fitzpatrick and Worthington were to find, as Jack Harris did, that Carver's influence would be felt throughout their lives. All three shared a similar pattern:

- losing a capability as children;
- then honing other abilities as adults and using them to prosper and give back;
- to exceed others' expectations; and possibly to exceed their own.

Jack T. Harris

There was a peace and a sense of fulfillment in both men. There were no regrets. There were no hard feelings about the cards they had been dealt. Although both men saw their world from wheelchairs, there was no doubt that their views were from a special and rare mountain-top. Their minds were sharp and their hearts filled with goodness and compassion – something we all should enjoy.

When both were alive, a reunion should have been arranged between the two men. Candidly, I should have made that happen. There might have been a major problem, however, and people from Alabama will appreciate the issue here. Tom was from the University of Alabama – Roll Tide; James was from Auburn University – War Eagle. Some things just cannot be reconciled!

We have learned from two men who benefitted from their being treated by Carver. But, we have not yet learned from Jack.

"Treat a man as he is,
and he will remain as he is.
Treat a man as he could be, and
he will become what he should be."

Ralph Waldo Emerson

Jack Seeking Adulthood

VIII

Nurturing, Challenging and Growing Jack: 1935 to 1940

The Carver-Ward friendship assumed a new dimension when the men entered into a unique, joint venture in 1935: growing Jack Harris.

Carver had treated Jack for polio symptoms prior to Jack's admission to Ward's school; Ward's involvement seems to have reinforced Jack's sense of well being and further invigorated the ties between Carver and Ward. They were tackling demanding work schedules in the five years they worked with Jack, but kept his health, education, and progress their priorities despite the hectic times.

Once again, grand old letters exchanged between Harris the boy, Ward the teacher, and Carver the scientist allow us to understand the journey they took together and the bonds they shared.

Jack's strained, irregular handwriting, found in his correspondence archived at Tuskegee University, takes effort to read and must have taken diligence and perseverance to produce. His desire to show his mentors that he was making progress and appreciation for their attention shines through in his words.

You will see Carver's endearing salutations to Jack in the sequences to follow; they gave this book its title. More so, for a young lad to actually write as he does to his mentor and for these letters to have been saved is a treasure of the highest kind. Let us enjoy this most amazing interaction through the "hot peanut oil" era.

Carver to Ward, October 1, 1936

My beloved friend, Principal Ward:

…I have just received a splendid letter from our boy, Jack Harris. He told me that he is improving, and that he has seen you and that you feel that he can come

Jack T. Harris

down from time to time. I have told Jack
right along that I knew that you would
do everything within your power for any
student in your school, that you were not
merely the Principal, but a real father
to each one. Jack really adores you,
and in this he shows such good sense.
I think there is a great deal to the boy,
and I shall be happy to continue doing
whatever I can for him. After the heavy
rain, I did not look for you yesterday.

Very sincerely yours, G. W. Carver

"There is a great deal to the boy."

Ward to Carver, October 5, 1936

My dear Dr. Carver:

I am just in receipt of your letter of
October 1. I went to Montgomery on the
30th of September but found it incon-
venient to take Jack Harris to Tuskegee
with me. I had to spend the entire day in
Montgomery. I am trying to devise some
way to get back to you from time to time.
We notice a great improvement over this

boy and I am sure that you will do him a
great deal of good. I can think of no man
within the circle of my acquaintance that
is doing the work, which you are doing.
With kindest regards,

Yours very truly, Lyman Ward

Carver to Ward, October 7, 1936

My beloved friend, Principal Ward:

…I am very glad that you notice a
decided improvement in our dear boy,
Jack. He impresses me, as I have said
before, as such a splendid young fellow
that it is a great pleasure to do what little
I have done for him. I shall look forward
to seeing him as often as it is convenient
for him to get down, as I believe that
through the providence of the Almighty
that he can be made whole. Your work
for humanity has always been a source
of inspiration to me.

Very sincerely yours, G. W. Carver

Harris to Carver, October 9, 1936

Dear Dr. Carver,

Jacob T. Harris

I am coming along fine with the peanut
oil. My arms and legs seem a lot better.
Most of the students that were here last
year have told me I was a lot better this
year. That makes me feel good as well
as I know there must be some change
in myself. I want to get over as soon as
I can but with Dr. Ward gone I can't get
things as straight as if he were here. The
soreness has not bothered me lately. I rub
both legs and my left arm every night.
My fingers are not as stiff as they were.
I notice in typing my hands are easier to
work the keys. My left thumb still wants
to double up, but I am rubbing and it
helps.

Yours very truly, Jack Harris

"I rub both legs and my left arm every night."

Carver to Harris, October 12, 1936

My dear boy, Jack:

I have enjoyed your letter very much.
You write splendidly and have quite a

literary air about your writing which
I am pleased to see. I hope you will
develop this quality. I am indeed happy
to learn that you are improving right
along, and you are improving in the
right direction. Just keep up the same
thing that you are doing until you can
get down to see me. You will have no
trouble to get off when the Principal
returns, as he has already told me that he
will arrange to have you get down every
so often, as he is thoroughly enthused
over your improvement. I hope that this
school year will be the most profitable
and pleasant of your experience.

Very truly yours, G. W. Carver

Ward to Carver, October 28, 1936

My dear Dr. Carver:

…We are greatly encouraged about
Jack Harris. He feels that you are a real
friend. I often think of your wonderful
gifts and of the distinct contribution,
which you have made to the well being

Jack T. Harris

of Alabama and to the world. May God
give you strength.

Yours very truly, Lyman Ward

Harris to Carver, October 28, 1936
(handwritten)

Dear Dr. Carver,

...The muscles of my legs seem to be
strong and are not sore at all. At first
they were sore all the time. Dr. Ward
said you were going to cure me and I told
him that I know it as you have helped me
so much now. I am enjoying this school
year better than ever.

Best wishes, Jack Harris

Carver to Harris, October 31, 1936

My dear boy, Jack:

Your fine letter has just reached
me and brings the usual amount of
enthusiasm and interest. I am so glad
to learn that you continue improving. I
really expected this, as you are doing
a fine piece of work for yourself, and

along with what I can do for you, I am confident that you are going to continue improving until you get entirely well. Just remember that the Great Physician will cooperate with us and bless the means employed to the healing thereof in all our work.

Very sincerely yours, G. W. Carver

Carver to Ward, October 31, 1936

My beloved friend, Principal Ward:

…Thank you for your fine letter. One came in the same mail from our dear boy, Jack Harris. It is a splendid letter and written by a real boy in whom is much promise. He is very enthusiastic over his improvement. With the full cooperation that he is giving me, and by keeping in touch with the great creative power and the Great Physician who can do all things, I am very certain that he can be made well.

Very sincerely yours, G. W. Carver

Jacob T. Harris

Harris to Carver, December 11, 1936

Dear Dr. Carver,

...I notice my thumb is standing out better.

Very truly yours, Jack T. Harris

Carver to Harris, December 14, 1936

My dear boy, Jack:

...I am certainly delighted to know that your thumb is beginning to straighten out, because it is these little things that determine the value of continued treatment. ...Keep up the massage exercises every day, that is, just exercise and rub the afflicted parts so as to give those muscles that need it the exercise needed for their development, and then begin feeding them the oil as soon as you return.

Very truly yours, G. W. Carver

Harris to Carver, April 4, 1937

Dear Dr. Carver,

…I regret that I missed you Friday
the 26th of March. I spent a long time
waiting for you at your room but you
did not come. Some of the boys said you
would be there soon and I waited. It will
be this summer before I get to see you
it looks like. …I am keeping up my oil
treatments and will continue.

Yours very truly, Jack T. Harris

Harris to Carver, May 4, 1937

Dear Dr. Carver,

…I have just finished rubbing my body
with the oil. I seem to be having good
luck with it. My teachers say I write
better. I sure hope I will make good
grades. I am really studying hard cause
I want to make good in future life. I am
always glad to hear things of interest
about you.

Yours very truly, Jack T. Harris

---

*"I am really studying hard cause I
want to make good in future life."*

Jack T. Harris

Harris to Carver, June 9, 1937

Dear Dr. Carver,

...I sure did enjoy the unveiling of your Bust last week. My friend did too. We just did get there on time. You were so busy till I did not get to let you give me a treatment.

Yours truly, Jack T. Harris

Harris to Carver, October 31, 1937

Dear Dr. Carver,

...My schoolwork is good. I was one of twelve students to make above 90 on the studies. We were on the stage. Everyone says I am improving ever so much. They think it fine that I play football. I still use the oil but not like I should I guess.

Yours very truly, Jack T. Harris

Carver to Ward, March 28, 1938

My beloved friend, Dr. Ward:

...Dr. Ward, I wish that you would give our boy, Jack Harris, as much attention as you can with reference to his disability. He has made great improvement and he can do much more.

Very sincerely yours, G. W. Carver

Carver to Harris, October 1, 1938

My dear boy, Jack:

...I am yet in the hospital, but am beginning to show some definite signs of improvement, which naturally come slowly. Keep up the oil massaging, and as soon as I am able to see you, I shall do so.

Very sincerely yours, G. W. Carver

Harris to Carver, October 14, 1938

Dear Dr. Carver,

I hope you are much better now. I was so glad to hear you are improving. Read the article in the paper I am sending on Boy Scouts. Dr. Ward asked me to write that and he published it. Also I am sending

Jacob T. Harris

a snapshot of me. I have often thought
I would send you one. I am doing
well with the oil. We play Tuskegee in
football October 28 at Tuskegee. Would I
be able to stop by and say hello to you if
I can get out there?

Very truly yours, Jack. T. Harris

Carver to Harris, October 17, 1938

My dear boy, Jack:

Thank you so much for your splendid
letter. I am glad to know that you are
going to play Tuskegee on the 28th of
October. I am yet in the hospital but feel
pretty sure that I will be strong enough
to see you at that time. They allow me
out every day now for just a little walk
and I am enjoying it very much. Please
remember me to President Ward and
tell him to continue his prayers as they
are having their results. I am so glad
that you sent me a copy of the Industrial
Student with your article. It is very
enlightening and well done. Most of all,
I am so pleased to get your fine picture.
I must say that you have developed

wonderfully, really a handsome boy, and I shall be looking for you when you come. I am most

Sincerely and gratefully yours, G. W. Carver

Carver to Harris, November 1, 1938

My dear boy, Jack:

…It certainly was good to see you the other evening. I confess I was greatly surprised to see the improvement that you had made. To me it is most gratifying and I trust that you will keep up your massage with the oil. I think it nothing short of wonderful that you are actually playing football.…I am pleased also to see that you are developing not only physically but in your intellectual appearance.

So sincerely yours, G. W. Carver

Harris to Carver, February 5, 1939

Dear Dr. Carver,

Jacob T. Harris

...When Mr. Scott left, I was in charge of the dormitory until another coach could be contacted. I have been very busy.... Dr. Carver, I am playing basketball. I enjoy the exercise and I believe it helps me...I am very anxious to get over to see you. I would like you to look me over and see if I have improved by doing as you tell me. ...I saw in the paper that you were back at work and it made me feel very good to know you were out. I am very interested in your health and want you to take care of yourself.

Very truly yours, Jack Harris

Harris to Carver, April 16, 1939

Dear Dr. Carver,

I read of the President's visit to see you and the school. I know it was quite an honor to you both to meet. I have had the pleasure of meeting you both and I am very fond of both. The occasion must have been a delightful one. I would like to have gone over but was unable. I seem to be doing fine but I believe if it were possible for me to see you I would be better. Some time in the near future I hope that I may see you. Dr. Ward sends his regards to you.

Very truly yours, Jack. T. Harris

Carver to Harris, April 18, 1939

My dear boy, Jack:

…I haven't as yet regained my strength but I am feeling some better. Naturally I would have been so happy to have seen my dear boy Jack.

Sincerely yours, G. W. Carver

Carver to Harris, June 17, 1939

My dear boy, Jack:

…Thank you very much for your letter. As yet my strength has not returned sufficiently for me to see but very few people and then for only a short time, but I am gradually on the upward trend I hope. …There may be someone here as there is scarcely a time when someone is not waiting to see me and I naturally see as many as I can which now is very few,

Jack T. Harris

and must be done very briefly. I shall
be glad to see you at your convenience
whenever you come.

Most sincerely yours, G. W. Carver

Harris to Carver, April 19, 1940

My dear Dr. Carver:

…This being my last year in high school,
I am having heavy work. Just yesterday
I finished a thousand word essay on
William Penn. It is being corrected
now—then I must learn it and give it
before the school. This is an annual
event of the senior class. … Several of
your students in electricity have been
here checking the wiring of our new
school building. I asked them if you
were out and they said yes. This was a
very pleasing report to me I can assure
you. Dr. Ward and I speak of you often
and we are always happy to hear of you
improving. Due to your fine work on me,
I have someone tell me of the improve-
ments in my walk and actions, almost
every day. They think you have proved
wonders on me and you really have, of

course they can't have the appreciation
I have. I only wish I could see you often
but that is impossible as it seems. …Even
if you couldn't work on me, I would
like to go by and see you. I want you to
see how your work has helped me. Next
year, I plan to study Forestry in some
college and I may be quite a distance
away, therefore I want you to look me
over. The Booker T. Washington stamp
occasion was interesting to me. They
sure paid honors to a truly great man. I
enjoyed the write-ups they gave you and
I am keeping them with the pictures.
Next I want to see a stamp in your honor.
Write me and let me know if at some
time I might come over.

Very truly yours, Jack T. Harris

Carver to Harris, April 22, 1940

My dear boy, Jack:

How happy I was to get your fine letter.
I have thought about you so very often
when I was really able to think. I have
been at a point where thinking was
impossible as three times they had

Jacob T. Harris

given up on me as ever being able to
survive, but I am able now to get to the
office both mornings and afternoons for
a little while enough to look after the
mail and afternoons for a little while
that I have to, that is, pressing needs. I
suggest you write me ahead of time, say
a week before you hope to come, as I
am yet under very strict medication and
I have to cooperate with my physician
in every way, and if he says no I can't
see anybody, of course, that shuts it off
. The weak heart is my main trouble but
it is gradually getting a little bit stronger
as I observe definite rules. I am so glad
that you are improving and that you are
coming up, as I do want to look you over
and it may be that I can point out some
things I want you to do. People still
come to me but I can't do any massaging
as yet, but I can tell them as best I can
what to do and some of them are getting
remarkable results and don't fail to come
and tell me about it. I shall be glad to see
you whenever you can come down, and
of course with the doctor's permission,
which I will have if I get a little notice

ahead. With so much love and best
wishes, I am

Most sincerely yours, G. W. Carver

Harris to Carver, October 29, 1940
324 Dolly Avenue, Missoula, Montana

My dear Dr. Carver:

At last I am doing the thing I wanted to
do for some time. I often think of you. I
came out here in July soon after I graduated from Camp Hill. You see I picked
Montana State University to attend and
I came out to see if I could get a job and
locate a board job during the school
year. Four days after I arrived here I
found a job in a cafe and worked my way
up. When school opened September 30,
I quit that job and started working for
my board here where I room. I also have
a job at the University, which takes care
of my room rent and a little over. At the
University I work in the Library and here
at the house I wash for my landlady and
scrub, I really enjoy my extra work even
though all my time is taken up. After
arriving in Montana, I changed my plans

Jack T. Harris

and as a result am taking Journalism.
My plans were to take Forestry but there
is a great deal of drawing connected
with Forestry and I seem to have trouble
there. However, the Journalism is a great
course. Please write me and let me know
how you are. I trust and hope you are up
and able to enjoy your work. I am very
sorry I have not been able to see you for
such a long time. What you have done
for me is wonderful. I am so much better
in every way. I can never forget it. People
here think it is interesting that I know
such a great and noted person as you.
If you have any suggestions you think I
should carry out please tell me. Dr. Ward
has written me several letters. He is
such a fine man. I truly miss being in his
school. My brother is in Auburn again
this year.

Very truly yours, Jack T. Harris

Carver to Harris, November 1940

My dear boy, Jack:

Imagine my surprise upon receiving
your fine letter and noting that you are

away out in Montana and that I will not
have the privilege of seeing you possibly
for a long time. It was so good of you
to write me and to let me keep in touch
with you. I am pleased to say that it
seems now that I will be able to get the
major part of my strength back again
as I am now able to walk around some
and be at the office both mornings and
afternoons for several hours at a time. I
am indeed pleased that you have a good
position and that you are out there where
you may be able to do still better by and
by. I am perfectly confident that you are
going to do your very best, and that your
best will be backed up by education and
your ability to do. I know that Dr. Ward
is most happy to know that you are so
well located. With hope that I will hear
from you from time to time, I am

Most sincerely yours, G. W. Carver

---

*It was 1940, the year of Jack's graduation from The
Southern and his first year off to college. That year, Dr.
Ward wrote an article about Jack. It is my understanding from Cullen Harris that Ward wrote these words so
that Jack's story could inspire others. The writing is*

Jack T. Harris

*especially poignant because it was written by the man
who had admitted Jack to The Southern, realizing that
the requirements might be too challenging for a young
man for whom the picking of peas in the field would
likely prove impossible.*

Lyman Ward on Jack Harris

"I read nearly every day of some deed of valor.

"My story is of one individual who in his waking
moments is performing deeds of valor. This is the story
of a boy who has not yet reached his majority.

"Now this lad has graduated with honor last May. He is
altogether the most courageous boy that I have ever had
to deal with. We sometimes say in a poetic way that life
is a conquest. Every waking hour there has been something for this boy to conquer. He has learned to walk
with assurance that he did not know when he came to
S.I.I. He can march with our youth in various exercises.
He has developed strength.

"Few boys can pull a steady load more surely than he.

"He has been the leader of our Boy Scouts and in the
project of erecting our log cabin clubhouse, he has been
a leader. In putting the heavy, slippery pine logs in place
we could not keep him on the ground. He was up on
staging or astride the log that was peeled, helping to get
it in place.

"Nothing ever fazed him.

"I remember the story of the great American Preacher Philips Brooks. Brooks had an impediment in his speech. When he confided to a friend that he had in mind to enter the ministry, this friend countered with the remark that the ministry was a closed profession to him because of the impediment that he could not rise above.

"So my valorous boy would learn to speak and have part in debates. I gave him only the simplest rules when he came for advice. I cautioned him to speak slowly and distinctly, enunciating every word and on his life he was to sit down the instant he became confused. I remember the morning he gave an essay for graduation before our assembly. How fine he looked with his forehead just about perfect and he made for himself a chin sufficiently protruding for one to know that he was really master of himself.

"This summer he paid me a visit, requesting a transcript of his grades. He was preparing to enter a great university in the Northwest. He was leaving his mother and all his loved ones to make his own way. An air-mail letter is upon my desk. Some way he had reached the college town. He found employment immediately and already has a nest egg in the way of savings and begins his college course this fall.

Jacob T. Harris

"I am writing this under much restraint. I must not make too much of him.

"In my present mood, I can think of no greater hero in the olden times than this lad in this day of nineteen and forty. Icarus flew toward the sun and would have reached that planet had not the heat melted the wax that held the wings to his body. This lad lives in our work-a-day world and not in the days of fable. Icarus, I am sure, had not more courage than the lad who has begun the long climb.

"In that temple of learning whither he has gone, I am sure that his valor will bring fresh luster to its renown."

Prophetic echoes of "Invictus": Ward realized that Jack had become "the master of himself"...the master of his soul. Just as Lyman Ward labored at exercising emotional restraint in his tribute to Jack, I'll do the same with regard to the significance of Ward's tribute. Ward's reflections only became available as my work on this book neared the finish; yet its insights elevated, elucidated, and affirmed so much of "My Dear Boy, Jack."

My research hit a wall at the year 1940. The Carver-Ward-Harris letters had been my compasses to date, but the well dried up in 1940. It would take more digging to learn whatever had happened to my dear boy, Jack.

As I thought long and hard about the young man seeking adulthood in 1940, I wondered who was Jack

Harris? I listened to his brother, his son, and persons associated with him at various times of his life, and dug more deeply into his chosen words. There were many whys not answered. In considering all elements of his life at this time, I made a decision not supported by evidence, so to speak – I knew what was most important – I knew his heart and soul. Technology and more interviews were not needed for me to drive on. After all, this was not intended to be a book – just the telling of a story around a fireplace in January with the warmth of the logs filling all the gaps.

Jack was no different from any of us, as we each have gifts, which mature within at different times, different periods – in the best or worst of times. I could not wait to follow this cluttered path, covered with brush that made it hard to discern where the next footprints led.

In the meantime, it had become evident that the two historic figures who had known and befriended Jack made for a riveting tale in themselves. As epic figures sought Carver's attention, Jack hovered on the edge of these relationships, close to Carver's heart... and even closer to Ward's watch.

It is possible that while FDR and Henry Ford were beckoning Carver into rarefied circles, Jack helped keep his feet grounded.

Jack T. Harris

It should be understood that both Carver and Ward were making quite a name for themselves. Few in Alabama really knew of the friendship and respect. But there was one fact known far and wide by two leaders in America that Carver was one of the very few scientists who was making a difference with polio – Ford and FDR.

"A mentor is an older, more experienced person who seeks to further the development of character and competence in a younger person... the mentor and the young person develop a special bond of mutual commitment. In addition, the young person's relationship to the mentor takes on an emotional character of respect, loyalty, and identification."

Dr. Urie Bronfenbrenner

IX

The Who's Who?:
Carver's Relationships with
Henry Ford and FDR

To my knowledge, Henry Ford never met Jack Harris.
However, what is important here is to appreciate how
Carver's life involved very important people, and yet he
took the time for one little boy. It also illustrates that
in the midst of a crisis, America needed Carver in the
worst way and yet, Carver seemingly placed no greater
priority on power or money from others, than he did on
the cry for help of a boy in pain.

Franklin D. Roosevelt did meet Harris. Jack Harris writes of it and Jack's brother, Cullen, and other information I uncovered confirms their meeting.

The world's top automaker and the President of the United States greatly admired Carver and sought out his advice and company. In fact, in Dearborn, Michigan, as a tribute to Carver, Ford installed a replica of the Missouri slave cabin in which Carver had been born.

Henry Ford

Ford intrigued and influenced Carver. Each seemed to appreciate the inventiveness of the other, and they shared a passion for science. In *The Fords, An American Epic,* authors Peter Collier and David Horowitz touch on another aspect of Ford that could have reinforced the friendship. They write that Ford "...stood for the populist values that grass-roots Americans believed in, values which were increasingly under assault in the modern world."

Henry Ford's father instilled in him a robust love of nature that lasted his lifetime, possibly one of the most compelling reasons he sought out Carver, whose affinity with nature approached the spiritual. The following quote is taken from Glenn Clark's book *The Man Who Talks with the Flowers,* and provides engrossing insight into Carver's bonds with nature. Carver observes, "Nature keeps telling me more and more of God. I go

Jack T. Harris

into the woods for hours and listen to the great secrets of God. One day after I returned from the woods something kept telling me, 'Go back, go back. You haven't got it all yet.'"

In the last seven years of Carver's life, he and Henry Ford were especially close, exchanging frequent and detailed communications. They inspired each other. Ford invested a good deal of energy in the relationship and evidenced obvious admiration and concern for the scientist. Once more, letters say it best.

Henry Ford's Assistant, Frank Campbell, to Carver,

April 11, 1939

Dear Dr. Carver:

...I am sending you recent snapshots of the Colored Community School, which is under construction near Ways, Georgia. Mr. Ford has expressed a desire to let this school be known as the George Washington Carver School, provided you have no objection to his doing so.

Sincerely yours, Frank Campbell

Carver to Ford, July 31, 1940

My great inspiring friend, Mr. Ford:

This is just to extend to you greetings upon your recent 77th Birthday
Celebration. I am feeling, successfully,
that I am improving physically, slowly
but surely. I am following your direc-
tions that you gave me at Ways, Georgia,
and there isn't any doubt about their
efficiency.

With kindest regards and best wishes
to Mrs. Ford, I am Most sincerely and
gratefully yours, George Washington
Carver

Ford to Carver, August 4, 1940

Dear Dr. Carver:

Thank you for the kind expressions
contained in your letter of July 31. I
appreciated hearing from you and am
pleased to know that you are feeling
much better.

Sincerely yours, Henry Ford

Jack T. Harris

Ford to Carver, August 5, 1940

Dear Dr. Carver:

Please accept my sincere thanks for
your friendly birthday greetings. It was
a pleasure to hear from you, and I am
happy to learn of your improved health.
With the very best wishes of Mrs. Ford
and myself.

Sincerely yours, Henry Ford

Ford to Carver, April 25, 1941

Dear Dr. Carver:

I wish you to know how much I enjoy
your letters, and trust you will continue
writing me from time to time. Your
welcome suggestions and the scientific
problems you have discussed are interesting and worthwhile discoveries, and
I have taken much pleasure in looking
over the various samples you forwarded.
It is gratifying to learn that your strength
is improving daily. Extending to you best
wishes of Mrs. Ford and myself.

Sincerely and respectfully, Henry Ford

Carver to Ford, February 4, 1942

My dear Mr. Ford:

…I want you to know also that the lifesaver (an elevator) you gave me is still performing its very unusual and efficient service and is proving a real life saver. With hope that nothing will prevent you from coming down this spring, I am

Most sincerely and gratefully yours, G. W. Carver

Ford to Carver, Western Union, March 6, 1942

Dr. G. W. Carver: Did you have a good trip home and how do you feel?

Henry Ford

"How do you feel?"

Ford could not hold back his concern for Carver. He was very concerned about Carver's health! So much so, that he sent a telegram when Carver left him, and it was waiting for Carver when he returned to Tuskegee.

Jacob T. Harris

Carver to Ford, March 23, 1942

To the greatest of all living prophets, Mr. Henry Ford:

...First, this is to extend to you and Mrs. Ford greetings and tell you how impossible it is for either of you to know, even in a small way, what this visit has meant to me personally. ...I am so inspired and enthused over your visit that I cannot write more at this time.

Most sincerely and gratefully yours, G. W. Carver

Carver to Mrs. Ford, March 30, 1942

My esteemed friend, Mrs. Ford:

...With the hope that the day is as beautiful there as here. Believe it or not, but I always feel better after a visit with you and Mr. Ford. I gather so much inspiration and enthusiasm to go ahead.

Most sincerely and gratefully yours, G. W. Carver

From 1938 to 1943, Ford and Carver exchanged at least fifty letters, visited each other in Dearborn and Tuskegee, and held each other's confidences. Professional interests factored into the mix: Ford sought Carver's help with projects at the Ford Research Center. The industrialist offered him a job, but Carver chose yet again to remain at Tuskegee. Shared interests glued the friendship, notably advances in agriculture and the study of nature.

As much as any other factor, though, an abiding concern for each other appears to have linked the two. Ford had special shoes made for Carver so his feet would not hurt. He gave him an elevator to spare stress on Carver's heart when walking up stairs. At one point, Ford wanted Carver at an important press gathering but out of concern for Carver's health, postponed the event for months so that Carver could stand with him and Mrs. Ford. Their letters clearly burst from the heart.

I recall reading in the Carver papers about the evening that Carver was to speak to a very large gathering in Dearborn, Michigan – a gathering of the nation's scientists. It was to be a formal dinner and when Carver arrived, he entered through the kitchen entrance. When he saw the formality and that Ford had placed him, as guest speaker, next to himself at the head table, Carver retreated back to the kitchen and asked if he might eat there. Ford was beside himself and insisted otherwise. Carver said, "No." Confused, Ford finally accepted

Jacob T. Harris

his friend's decision. When the meal was nearly over, Carver joined the others in the great hall. The all-white scholars stood and greeted him with complete acceptance and Carver delivered a brilliant speech on the role of science in America. Afterward, Ford and Carver walked into the woods a way, sat on an old fallen tree, and just talked. There is no record of the conversation.

Carver always kept the common touch as he walked with kings. For several of the years that he maintained a friendship with Ford, he was regularly treating Jack Harris for polio symptoms.

Franklin D. Roosevelt

Carver was assisting another polio victim at this time too, an especially famous one; President Franklin Delano Roosevelt. It's highly likely that Jack Harris might have taken some pride in knowing that he and the president were both special to Carver and each benefited from his care and counsel.

Carver and Roosevelt were not close friends but they were in communication and the mutual respect was obvious.

Roosevelt to Carver, December 30, 1936

Dear Dr. Carver:

I wish to join many friends in recogniz-
ing your achievements in behalf of your
fellow men. I know something of your
influence in the field of science and your
constant inspiration to associates and
friends. Your work has been indispens-
able in shaping the agricultural activities
of the Tuskegee Normal and Industrial
Institute, with which you have been
associated as Director of Agriculture for
many years. Your faith in human nature,
your ability to see the good about you
and to lend a directing hand to talent
where it needs stimulating, are at the
very basis of your life's work.

Very sincerely yours, Franklin D.
Roosevelt

*"Your faith in human nature, your
ability to see the good about you
and to lend a directing hand to talent
where it needs stimulating, are at
the very basis of your life's work."*

Jack T. Harris

Carver to Roosevelt, April 4, 1939

Honorable Sir:

This is just to extend to you greetings,
and to thank you again and again for
your visit to Tuskegee Institute and
giving me the rare privilege of shaking
the hand of one of the truly great characters of the world, statesman, diplomat,
and a great humanitarian. If you are not
already doing it, I beg of you to have
your Physio-therapist use pure peanut
oil. I so thoroughly believe it will help
you in connection with your splendid
hydro-therapy treatment.

So gratefully yours, Geo. W. Carver

Roosevelt to Carver, April 7, 1939

My dear Dr. Carver:

I am grateful to you for your note and
happy, too, that I had the privilege of
meeting you at Tuskegee last week.
Yours has been and is a life of service of
which the American people are proud. I

do use the peanut oil from time to time and I am sure that it helps.

Very truly yours, Franklin D. Roosevelt

"I do use the peanut oil..."

Carver to Mrs. Roosevelt, March 14, 1941

My esteemed friend, Mrs. Roosevelt:

This is to extend to you greetings, and to say that I am informed that you plan to be in Tuskegee on the twenty-eighth of this month. I trust you will not be so rushed that you cannot see our Museum, and I do want to talk with you with reference to your honorable husband's disability, and show you some things that are very gratifying to me in the work, which I am attempting to do. With kindest regards to both yourself and Mr. Roosevelt, I am

Very sincerely yours, G. W. Carver

Jack T. Harris

Roosevelt to the United States

The White House

January 15, 1943

(Ten days after Carver's death, President
Roosevelt made this dedication
announcement.)

"...I am delighted that the National
Foundation for Infantile Paralysis
is to be associated with this historic
institute...

Tuskegee is a perfect setting for a
hospital unit to care for infantile
paralysis victims. The roads to Tuskegee
are covered with travelers—on foot,
by oxen, on mules, by automobile and
train—relatives bringing their sick, the
lame—to be made well again. It takes
sacrifice and effort for them to come and
they make the trip with courage and they
are not disappointed. ...This new three-
story, thirty-five bed unit, is completely
equipped for the treatment and care of
the infantile paralysis patient...From this
new hospital center at Tuskegee, will
come a new knowledge and interest in
infantile paralysis and we hope for a new

and ever-widening program which will further our efforts in the conquest of this disease."

As history would have it, not only did Carver know Roosevelt, but his dear boy Jack did as well. Harris met Roosevelt on more than one occasion, according to Jack's brother, Cullen. In one instance, March 30, 1939, Jack and the president conducted a military review together at A.P.I. (Auburn University).

As I ventured forth in the pursuit of more information, something kept nagging at me – from past facts. It deals with Ford and Carver – their unlikely friendship. I understand Carver in pursuit, but it was Ford who kept the rally going. Ford simply could not do enough for his sickly friend and one of America's greatest scientists. In Carver, Ford believed and trusted.

During these days of piecing together the intersections of Jack Harris, Henry Ford, President Roosevelt, Carver, and Ward, another name surfaced on the radar screen – a name that linked Henry Ford to Jack Harris's school. An alumnus of The Southern, J. Anderson Blackburn, sold Ford automobiles in Opelika, Alabama, and Carver and Ward conspired behind the scenes to introduce Blackburn to the automaker, knowing it would be a rare treat. Carver and Ward never stopped doing good, until they stopped for good.

Jack T. Harris

"My best friend is one who
brings out the best in me."

Henry Ford

"We cannot always build the future
for our youth, but we can build
our youth for the future."

Franklin D. Roosevelt

X

J. Anderson Blackburn:
Lyman & George
Conspiring Once More

In trailing the arcs of the historical friendships that united Jack's mentor, George W. Carver, with other leading lights of his era, I came upon yet another special relationship that may qualify more in the category of "Who's He?" than "Who's Who."

A man named J. Anderson Blackburn came to my attention in a letter from Carver to Lyman Ward. Carver seemed to be working something out for Ward regarding Blackburn, but what it was remained a mystery.

Then, as luck would have it, I noticed a published story about J. Anderson Blackburn that pulled it all together. It ran in the "Opelika News" in the late 1930s.

I called a friend in Opelika, Dora James, who referred me to Henry Stern, long time resident and friend. During a visit I made to him, Stern mentioned, "You know, there was an old business in Opelika that had a picture of Henry Ford on the wall, with George Carver in it." The business was Opelika Tire Service, which was owned by Bobby Huling. The photo was a treasured stay-behind from Huling's father's business, and hung where it had always been.

Sure enough, the photo showed Ford and Carver, along with a third man, walking the Tuskegee grounds. On the back of the photo were three names; the third man was identified as J. Anderson Blackburn.

Next stop – the archives of the Auburn University Library, which harbored press clippings of Ford's visit; one article from March 19, 1938 and another, with photo, dated March 20, 1938. Later, I learned that Blackburn often told the story of the occasion. The story follows, as best I can weave it together:

What Carver and Ward together acted upon with Blackburn, is a case in point, in terms of how they treated others who had benefited from their lives' work.

Jack T. Harris

It was 24/7 with them, and no one was denied their care and support.

J. Anderson Blackburn had been a student of Dr. Lyman Ward at The Southern Industrial Institute around 1910. He later became the Ford dealer in Auburn, Alabama. He and Ward had kept in touch throughout the years and Ward was fond of him. When Henry Ford was planning one of his visits to see Dr. Carver and Tuskegee, Carver and Ward decided to introduce Blackburn to Ford, if at all possible. From what I could discern, the proposal was probably Ward's, with Carver agreeing and wanting to make it happen.

When the day arrived for Ford's visit with Carver in Tuskegee, an Associated Press reporter called Blackburn to ask him if would like to meet Henry Ford. Blackburn told him, "I am too busy selling his cars, and I do not have time today." Some thirty minutes later, the phone rang again and Blackburn was told a Ford limo would pick him up shortly.

In fifteen minutes, the limo arrived outside. Blackburn got in and was chauffeured over to a building at Tuskegee. He was ushered through several doors and came upon one protected by a guard. The door opened and Blackburn saw Carver and Ford sitting down. Ford got up, walked to the door and invited Blackburn in. They stood there talking about the Ford product. Henry Ford asked Blackburn what he thought of that year's model and Blackburn told him that he thought it needed some changes. Ford inquired further and Blackburn did not hold back. Fifteen minutes later, Blackburn looked at his watch, and excused himself, saying he had cars to sell.

Henry Ford reached for Blackburn's arm and asked him to stay for the day. From that moment, Blackburn and Ford talked about Ford automobiles all day long. Ford invited him to dinner with Dr. Carver and then to a special musical tribute in the chapel, where Ford sat between Blackburn and Carver. After the music, all bid good-bye and Blackburn was chauffeured back to Auburn.

We have two actual accounts of the day. One derives from a call from Blackburn to Ward the next day, with a blow by blow. The other is a newspaper account in the *Opelika-Auburn News* by an Associated Press reporter. The two differ on certain small details but it's definite that Blackburn got picked up and taken to Tuskegee to meet Ford for a short early meeting. When it appeared to Blackburn that the introduction and short visit were over, he made attempts to leave. That's when Ford grabbed his arm and requested that he remain for the day. Photographs taken that day show Blackburn touring the Tuskegee campus with Ford and Carver.

In wishing to learn more of Mr. Blackburn's life, I met and visited with his daughter, Ms. Christine Blackburn

Jacob T. Harris

Danner. As we spoke of her father, I was excited to learn about the man who had spent a day with Henry Ford and who had been a student of Lyman Ward.

She shared several stories, which I found of particular interest.

When she was a little girl in the 1920s in Opelika, Alabama, Anderson Blackburn was Opelika's Santa Claus. Her mother took her to meet Santa Claus downtown one Christmas, and when she did, she recognized her father's voice. That is how Ms. Danner learned the truth about Santa Claus.

During the period of 1930 to 1942, her father owned a newly-started Ford dealership in Auburn, Alabama. He held a citywide contest to name the business and the town voted for "Tiger Motor Company." Located on College Street in Auburn, the company's building still stands and is now used by various businesses.

Blackburn sometimes allowed a few of the football players and other athletes at Auburn University (then A. P. I.) to use his brand new demonstrator car on special "date" occasions. His name became "Coach Blackburn" and he actually traveled with the team on away games over a twelve-year period. Two of the players from that time were All-American Jimmie Hitchcock and Auburn's 1932 – Best All-Around Athlete, Ralph Jordan.

When Ms. Danner was a little girl, on Sunday after-noons, her father would drive the family in a new Ford automobile, to his favorite places. One of those places was The Southern Industrial Institute.

As to Blackburn's character, a dear friend of his, Emmett Sizemore, stated in a letter dated February 19, 1942, "Blackburn is a gentleman of high ideals, excellent character, integrity, and honest in his dealings. His strong point is handling hard situations on a high plane and in an up and up manner. I take great pleasure in giving this impression from many years of acquaintance and dealings."

On an even more personal note, Ms. Danner shared a letter from her father to her mother before they were married. It is dated February 16, 1919. From France while in the US Army, Blackburn wrote these words to his Vera, "I have spent lots of time away from my mother who has been one of the best mothers that any boy could have and she will not live forever. I feel like it is my duty to stay near her when I can. I know you would love her.... My heart has never left the dear old U. S. A. and I pray every day that soon the time will come that I can go back to the place I left and love and reward the one who has been so tenderly caring for it.... Lovingly yours, Anderson"

Lyman Ward knew and taught his students well. Having interviewed more than 100 of his former students, I

Jack T. Harris

have learned of a certain developed strength of charac-
ter, that these Americans feel was their primary learn-
ing experience under Ward's educational program. It is
of little wonder that Ward did what he did for one of his
boys. From this perspective, Blackburn and Harris had
much in common.

March 18, 1938 was hardly business as usual for J.
Anderson Blackburn, due to the combined forces of
Ward and Carver. Ms. Danner told me, "That one day
became the highlight of my father's work life and is certainly a family memory that is celebrated even still." The
treasures on the family wall underscored her remarks.
This was a family that loved the "dear old U.S.A."

The educator and the scientist never seemed to stop
thinking about their students, regardless of age. Even
as Jack moved on to new chapters after leaving their
circles, there's no doubt they would have helped again
if they could.

Jack Harris was off to build his dream but it would not
be without many obstacles, as nothing came easily for
Jack.

"The outward freedom that we shall attain
will only be in exact proportion to the
inward freedom to which we may
have grown at a given moment."

Gandhi

Photographs to Remember Jack By

Carver put great effort in answering
this mountain of letters (133 per day)
from all over the world – with letters
back to Jack being a priority, as Jack
dealt with his infantile paralysis

Infantile paralysis gripped the
nation in the 1930's with cripling
our children in the worst way!

There is an old saying that some
people were born to do what they do.
Lyman Ward was born to teach!

Carver was a scientist first and foremost.
When in his laboratory with multiple
experments, he was in his heaven!

Disabled or not, how could anoyone
not vote for this FDR smile as he
played in the pool at Warm Springs?

Fitzpatrick seemed most comfortable
with his disability, and lived his
life focused on his ABILITY!

Worthington looked the hollywood
type, and sang far better than most.

This photo was sent by Jack to
Carver to show how well he was
doing in 1939. Rather proud of his
progress was he. He should be.

Research and letters confirmed the
special relationship George Carver
and Henry Ford enjoyed. They not
only shared much, but they listened
and learned from one another.

There was a mutual respect by both
FDR and Carver for one another.

After much work behind the scenes,
Carver and Ward brought Blackburn
together with Ford at Tuskegee,
and Ford loved Blackburn's honesty
about the new Ford automobile.

There comes a time in everyone's
life when the best of them should be
recognized by others. This was well
deserved. (Jack is second from the left
receiving the award from the city of
Mobile. The only missing persons were
Ward and Carver, for obvious reasons.)

Rare it is to see one's life achievements presented in this fashion. Holding and reading each accomplishment was a real honor for the author. For Jack, it had to have been his thank you to Carver and Ward. One day this should be framed in the very place Jack built for Mobile youth.

Jack is shown reading to his children
at the Boy's Club in Mobile.

Jack, Jr. looked much like his father.

Jack, Sr. loved life, as his smile tells us so!

Jack Jr. Loved dogs as Jack Sr. did.

Cullen needed Jack. Jack needed
Cullen. Both needed their dog –
Peggy. In their teens, they were
everything to one another, and
only grew closer in later years.

Jack's Years of Changing
Young Lives for the Better

XI

Making Good:
The House That Jack Built

Life's lessons are continual and not always easy to accept. There was much yet for Jack to learn, experience and to continue his journey into the wild. There were no guarantees. There were no easy open doors to success. In his life, he had learned that knocking on a door he wanted so badly meant little.

It was time for Jack to be the master of his fate, with little assurance other than it was time to tackle life without the gainful nurturing of Ward and Carver. He no longer had them to turn to.

It was now time to learn who he was and what his life might become. He ventured forth and pursued his college dreams far away from Alabama.

After a few months, Jack was unable to continue his education at the University of Montana. After one year, he was back home in Montgomery, Alabama.

I could find no evidence of why Jack had to leave the university in 1941, and I wonder if it might have been that he no longer had the support of Ward and Carver at his side. We do know that his disability made it difficult for him to be in forestry. What we also know is that he came home with head in hand. Jack seemed to be embarrassed to admit failure to anyone – especially to Ward and Carver.

As with any of us facing failure square in the face, it becomes a matter of choice, of will, and of resilience. If Jack had learned anything in those years with his mentors, he probably learned how to bounce back, and more so, to thrive. For a while after his disappointment at the university, being a couch potato was his order of the day, but not for long.

Cullen Harris remembers that Jack was saddened by this turn of events, sensing that his disability was influencing his future. He even questioned his intellectual skills and felt that he was failing and disappointing those who had been there for him, mainly Carver and Ward.

Jack T. Harris

Cullen recalls,

"At one point, Jack lay around the house doing nothing, saddened by it all. We each waited him out. But finally, Mother had enough and gave Jack a 'talking to.' Although Jack was ready to get back up one more time, he needed to hear what she had to say. Shortly thereafter, in 1941, Jack set out to prove himself - on his own, to make his way in life again. When he left home this time, it was to make good – for good."

He made his way to the city of Mobile, Alabama, where he would live and work for the rest of his life. From 1941 to 1955, Jack apparently required no more "talking to." He went to work with all the skills he did have and made a life for himself, compensating for the abilities he did not have.

It would appear that a formal education was not in the cards for Jack. This was hard for him to swallow, but he would find a way – his own way in his own time.

The education he had received from Ward and Carver just might be enough for him to help others. After all, what we do know is that he had the heart and resiliency to bounce back after falling again and again.

This was so much the case, that further research uncovered a document not to be believed. Talk about bouncing back, consider this:

A proclamation from the city of Mobile, Alabama, declared March 13, 1978, "Jack T. Harris Day."

What? In 1978, thirty-seven years after his failure in Montana – Jack was being honored with a day dedicated to him!!! What had he done to deserve this?

The decree addressed Jack's life from 1941 to 1955 and read,

> "Whereas, Jack T. Harris has devoted his entire life to the guidance of boys, having worked with the YMCA in Montgomery, Alabama, and in Missoula, Montana; and having worked in Scouts in Missoula, Montana and in Camp Hill, Alabama; and was the first employee with the City of Mobile Recreation Department, opening its first recreation center and serving as its Director; and having assisted in planning and building the Spring Hill Avenue Recreation Center and serving as its Director; and having supervised many playgrounds…"

The proclamation continued to extol Jack's accomplishments in youth programs – his passion. As I held the proclamation, I wished that Ward and Carver could have been there. It was they who should have been

Jack T. Harris

holding this evidence of what they worked together to help make good.

By 1955, Jack had become the Executive Director of the Boy Scout program in Mobile. His son noted in an August 2004 interview, "Pop headed up the Boy Scouts in Mobile for twenty-two years." Jack's involvement in scouting dated back at least to his student days at The Southern, where he was a scout leader from 1935 to 1940.

Since that time, Jack had evidently thought hard about youth programs and rose to a position from which he could bring about transformation in Mobile. He had listened and watched during his years with Ward and Carver and he had a torch to carry as he morphed from protégé to mentor. His sense of responsibility was keen.

But deep within, something was gnawing at Jack. He was not satisfied with what he was doing to help Mobile's youth. He could do more. He wanted to do more. He knew better. He knew what few did – in Mobile, Alabama.

It was a progressive city with wonderful leadership, and Jack knew it was time to tap those visionary leaders with an idea.

It was almost as if Jack was presaging Henry Ford's marketers, as he had a "better idea." And he called upon his past network of relationships to pursue a larger dream. The Boy Scouts were well situated. The Mobile recreation program was highly effective.

But Jack knew that there was one program that could fulfill a need neither of the other two could. But, Jack sensing opportunity where few were could not get the black youth of Mobile to join the scout program. He could not get black youth to join in with white youth in recreational programs. Street gangs were developing and Jack sensed that he needed to act.

It was time for Jack to use all that he had learned from Ward and Carver and put it to work, in spite of the highly unsettling racial issues in Alabama. Jack would have none of it.

As master of his fate, he acted, starting with a letter to an old friend.

Jack explained his plans to launch a Boys' Club, to J. Brackin Kirkland, who had graduated from The Southern in 1912. After later graduating from Cornell University, Kirkland had become an executive with the Boys' Club of America, in New York. In 1942, he left the Boys Club to return to The Southern in Camp Hill, Alabama, as its second president, succeeding none other than Dr. Ward.

I sought more information – there had to be more letters somewhere.

Jack T. Harris

The following letters were found in the University of Southern Mississippi Archives, in the J. Brackin Kirkland Papers.

Harris to Kirkland, September 29, 1955

Dear Mr. Kirkland,

It has been a long time since seeing or hearing from you. Hope everything is going swell with you. I haven't forgotten my talks with you and now I want to ask you a favor. For ten years I have been talking about the need of a boy's program in Mobile. Now looks like I have a chance to get the backing to put it over. So much is being said on Juvenile Delinquency, plus all the Civic Clubs, the Police, and others are coming up with ideas. I am getting together infor-mation now and have a group I believe will help to put it over. They back my Scout program. I know you have worked with many groups and thought you might have some literature you would loan me. Anything you have on organization, program planning, building operation, or any ideas you can give me, I will appreciate.

Yours truly, Jack T. Harris

Kirkland to Harris, October 11, 1955

Dear Jack,

…News of you and your accomplishments are inspiring, especially to those of us who know how heroically you have carried on against odds that might have well ended your aspirations and promising future of service. The Scout Medal Award picture shows both maturity and resolute character and I am betting on you getting a Boys' Club in Mobile.

…By the way, Eugene Bottoms and his lovely wife stopped by on their vacation. He graduated, as you know from The Southern, then from the University of Alabama, did three years work for Masters' Degree with the Texas Oil Company in Houston. I mentioned your success and aspirations to him and he said that "Jack Harris worked fifty times harder that the rest of us to learn typing and I'll bet he has a Boys' Club

Jack T. Harris

if it takes him ten years to get it. He and
Roosevelt never accepted defeat."

...If I can't get the help from the national
organization, then you and I will find a
way. Should you prefer for any reason
for me to sit in with you or a few very
selected laymen please let me hear from
you, for success often depends on the
initial move.

...Keep in mind that among our most
outstanding industrialist's gifts in
Alabama, the Roberts brothers in Mobile
were the largest donors to The Southern.

...When you are ready to launch a real
Boys' Club, you can count on any help I
can give within limitations and without
any obligations on your part. All success
to you! Mrs. Kirkland joins me in best
wishes.

Sincerely yours, J. Brackin Kirkland

---

*Jack likely never knew that scribbled at the bottom of
this letter by Kirkland to Mr. William E. Hall, the president of the Boys' Clubs of America from 1918 to 1954
in New York, were these words, "Mr. Hall, This is for*

Ripley's Believe It or Not." Yes, this was most certainly a believe it or not!

Harris to Kirkland, October 17, 1955

Boy Scouts of America letterhead
Jack T. Harris, Scout Master

Dear Mr. Kirkland,

…This Wednesday, Troop 7 is having a party and we have several men coming. Malcolm McLean will be one of them, you know he is the man who bought Waterman Steamship Co. My committee is behind me and they want Mr. McLean to see the Troop and know some of my work.

…I will write Mr. Hall soon. I want to get together all material so I can lay it before this group. I have found the people of Mobile willing to go along with me and that would sure be helpful to get you here at the right time.

Sincerely, JTH

Attached to the letter was a document entitled "Proposed Boys' Club, submitted by Jack T. Harris." It began, "The

Jack T. Harris

purpose of this program will be to help boys grow into manhood and be useful citizens and to eliminate some of the much talked about JUVENILE DELINQUENCY in our City."

Kirkland to Harris, November 3, 1955

Dear Jack:

...It was especially reassuring to
learn that you and your committee are
effectively educating Mr. McLean,
who bought the Waterman Steamship
Company from Ed Roberts. With those
two men, plus J. P. Roberts, interested in
the project, your success is more nearly
assured." With every good wish for your
success.

Sincerely, J. Brackin Kirkland
cc: to Mr. Hall, NYC

Harris to Kirkland, December 30, 1955

Dear Mr. Kirkland:

...Things were lagging for a while but
these last two weeks have been booming.
I have had so much happen that I feel a
Boys' Club is in the making. I believe

the right people are interested now and the ball is rolling.

...All these men seem to have great confidence in me and I hope I can deliver it.

...I'm carried away with it all.

Sincerely, JTH

"I'm carried away with it all."

Harris to Kirkland, February 4, 1960

BOYS' CLUB of MOBILE, INC.
letterhead
Jack T. Harris, Club Director

Dear Mr. Kirkland:

...For a number of years *(five years later)*, I have intended writing you to let you know the progress that has been made in Boys' Club work in Mobile. You were a big help in getting me started in the right direction.

...You will note Boys' Clubs of Mobile is now a reality. I have operated our

first Club one year on a part time basis.
This past November first, our Board
of Directors moved into a full-time
operation. Already, the Kiwanis Club
has agreed to build a second unit in a
much-needed area. I am also working
with the Negro group and hope our third
Unit will get under way before too long.

Sincerely, JTH

Harris to Kirkland, April 27, 1966

Dear Mr. Kirkland:

...We seem to have lost contact with
each other and I guess simply because
we are both kept busy. I have talked
about you a great deal the last few years
and have intended writing many times.
In February, I attended a Regional
Executive Conference of the Southern
Region, Boys' Clubs of America, and
had several good talks with Walter Hall
of the New York Staff . He certainly has
the highest regards for you and never
fails to ask if I have seen or heard from
you.

Sincerely, JTH

Hinds to Harris, April 27, 1971

(A. Boyd Hinds was the National
Director of the Boys' Club of America)

Dear Jack:

…It was a very pleasant surprise to hear
from you the other morning, not only
because it was you writing but because
you sent me information about J. B.
Kirkland who was my former boss of
many, many years ago, and from whom I
had not heard for many years.

…When all is said and done, he was the
guy who hired me many, many, many
years ago, and this ought to please
anyone that he was complimentary of my
now being the National Director.

Cordially, A. Boyd Hinds

Harris to Kirkland, June 8, 1971

Dear Mr. Kirkland,

…My trip to Atlanta was very nice and
the convention was a great one. More
than 1,500 delegates attended from over

Jack T. Harris

the country, with Boys' Clubs of Canada
and Britain represented. It was of the
best held I am sure.

Sincerely, JTH

There is a gap in letters between 1978 and 1989. We know that the Boys' Club Jack founded blossomed and thrived. The scouts he led for twenty-two years, Troop 7, became part of the Boys' Club of Mobile in 1957. Mobile's Jack T. Harris Day celebrated the first twenty years of the Boys' Club's success. Like any successful organization, Harris's was the product of teamwork. He had a supportive and service-oriented team. Without Jack Harris and his dream, however, Mobile might not have the high-performing club it has today.

By 2013, the Mobile Club separated into three divisions: Boys & Girls Clubs of South Alabama, P.O.I.N.T.E. Academy, LLC and Youth Programs of South Alabama. Youth Programs is the parent company. They now operate six, year-round, chartered clubs, three summer sites in schools and a 150-acre day camp. It is part of a national network of 4000 clubs run by 42,000 trained professional staff members. It takes about $800-$1,000 per year, per child, with a membership of 250 per youth to operate a club.

With joy in his heart in the heavens above, Jack must be leaping to touch doorframes over this wonderful success story, which is led today by Mary Zoghby.

Many Jack Harrises from all over America have built the BGCA into the premier organization it is today.

In an August 2004 interview, Jack Jr. talked about his father's vision and perseverance. "My father lived and died for kids – kids in trouble, who needed someone. When kids were real problems, he would go anywhere to settle the problem.

"Back then; there were a few gangs, both black and white youth gangs. On at least two occasions that I remember well, Pop went out into the night to solve some disputes between gang members. On both occasions, Pop was beaten up pretty badly. They beat up my pop, who was disabled and trying to help them. When he came home, I was truly so hurt for him. He would have died for those boys; hell, he almost did. That was '54 and '55, and I was eight and nine years old. I will never forget that.

"Pop was beaten up pretty badly."

"Pop used to say, 'There is no such thing as a juvenile delinquent. They will be no better than the environment they grow up in. It is the parents who are delinquent in their responsibilities to the child.'"

Jacob T. Harris

Asked about his father's skills in coping with disability, as he established the Boys' Club of Mobile, Jack Jr. said:

"He absolutely did not tolerate adversity. To him, it had to be done. Walking was always a problem all of his life. He never tolerated people complaining; he never did and would not allow me to either. He never saw color and that was his way. He treated all people the same all the time. That was one thing you could depend on with Pop. He learned that from Carver and Ward in his young life.

"My pop built more than one house over this twenty-year period. He built the Boys' Club 'house' so to speak, but he built our house, board-by-board, nail-by-nail. I helped him as a boy and we built our house. Together, we were – just us."

Jack's brother, Cullen, also reflected on his brother's success. "Jack always had a view of himself that was different from what others saw in Jack. He, even as a teenager, considered himself to be the 'king of the roost.' That's what he thought he was and the way he considered himself.

"King of the Roost, he was!

"He did not like to see photos of himself that showed his disability. In his later years, when the disability was more obvious in photos, Jack hated to think that he looked like that because he never saw himself that way. That was Jack. That is why he overachieved, in my view.

"I can tell you from his boyhood to his later years, Jack always was 'king of the roost.'"

"King of the roost, he was."

The citizens of Mobile seemed to think Jack deserved the title, given his work for thousands of young people. From among the many news clippings over the years when Jack was "king of the roost," several were printed in the *Mobile Register.*

One had the headline:

Jack T. Harris Praised

We agree with Mayor Lambert Mims that you can't help but admire a person who has dedicated his life of 45 years to helping young people.

…An unassuming man, Harris reacted to the ceremony in his honor with these words, "I don't know why they did this. I've got to work harder now to deserve it." Well, we would point out that the honor paid this gentleman was well deserved and highly appropriate. There is no way of totaling the thousands of Mobile youngsters who have been

Jack T. Harris

guided toward a better citizenship by
this dedicated man.

In the same article, Jack was quoted,

"I can't get over this. These are the men who deserve
it, not me." Harris feels many parents should become
involved with their children. "It will take more work on
their part, but the reward will come back in later years.
After all, you can't raise yourself."

"After all, you can't raise yourself."

*Some truths are more emphatic because of their sim-
plicity. Jack's observation, "You can't raise yourself,"
is one. It is an adage for an age that increasingly
values parenting and mentoring skills. There are many
things that drive people to do what they do for their
livelihoods – or with their lives. When brother, Cullen
Harris, stated, "We were not wanted," when they were
little, this had to be a driving force behind Jack's life
and his empathy for those youths who may have been in
a similar place that Jack understood so well. How else
would he know?*

*Starting in 1981, Jack's official retirement year, he
served as a consultant to the organization he founded.
His polio symptoms had begun to manifest themselves
in ways difficult to ignore, as he grew older. His body
sent signals he had long remembered – signals that*

even, my dear boy, Jack could not deny, and this time – there would be no Carver and Ward nurturing and encouraging. The hot peanut oil treatments had had their day – but no more.

The "king of the roost" was being challenged once more – some forty to fifty years later.

Jacob T. Harris

"The ideal life is in our blood and never
will be still. Sad will be the day for
any man when he becomes contented
with the thoughts he is thinking and
the deeds he is doing - where there
is not forever beating at the doors
of his soul, some great desire to do
something larger, which he knows
that he was meant and made to do."

Phillips Brooks

Jack's Last Years

XII

Jack's Days Are Few:
Never Giving Up

The year is 1989.

Letters, letters, where are you? Surely, there will be more!

Though he's tried to live every day exceeding expectations, Jack is finding his body unwilling to cooperate to the extent it has in the past. There are pains – many pains. His difficulty in chewing is frustrating. Holding a pen to write is nearly impossible. His walking has become labored.

For Jack, maneuvering through each day is taking a toll. But the challenges do not stop him from fighting and planning; his strong suits.

His spirit was intact – from beginning to end, nothing would dampen his determination to change a life. It was done for him.

Once more, we have letters from Jack that best express his goals.

They are reflective, and he was beginning to reach out again to Lyman Ward's school. The Southern Industrial Institute had been renamed in 1955; it became Lyman Ward Military Academy. Ironically—maybe providentially—in that same year, Jack was realizing his own dream with the help of Ward's successor, J. Brackin Kirkland.

By age seventy, Jack was thinking about legacies for his alma mater and the Boys Club. References to a foundation, scholarship, and award, appear in his correspondence. The following notes and memoranda involving Jack and Lyman Ward Military Academy were handled under the direction of then-president, Albert Hovey.

Major General Clyde Hennies (retired) served as the academy's president in 2000-2003, during much of my research. With his permission, that of Jack T. Harris, Jr., and that of the Boys & Girls Club of South Alabama, I was able to secure and use the following documentation

Jack T. Harris

and file notes. Also, the Harris family provided personal letters sent by Jack in his last years.

Harris Phone Call with Lyman Ward Military Academy

April 6, 1989

"Harris advised the school that he was setting up a foundation upon his death that would include all of his property, total possessions, and home. The proceeds of the foundation are to be divided between The Boys Club of America, Mobile and Lyman Ward Military Academy."

Albert Hovey

Harris Phone Call with Lyman Ward Military Academy

November 9, 1989

He advised us that he had been in the hospital for about ten weeks. He has had surgery on a bone in his hip. Having an awful problem walking. He has taken out

an insurance policy so that the award he
has established will continue forever.

Albert Hovey

Harris to Lyman Ward Military
Academy

May 4, 1990 (handwritten)

...Thanks for a real great day - one of
the greatest. ...Dr. Ward would be so
pleased. ...Seeing schoolmates meant
much to me. All of this and your kind-
ness makes me know why I wanted to do
what I did with my will. ...The picture of
Dr. Ward brought back good memories.
It is just like him.

Yours, JTH

Lyman Ward Military Academy to
Harris

May 7, 1990

Dear Jack:

Jack T. Harris

...The award will be presented by the
Chairman of the Board of Trustees on
May 19th, 1990.

Albert Hovey

Harris to Lyman Ward Military
Academy

May 1, 1991 (handwritten)

...If I haven't said it before I must say it
here - I left in 1940 knowing I would one
day give something back. Well, I am.

My best to all of you, JTH

Well, I am!

*That says it all! He, like those before him, Jack gave
back.*

Establishment of the Jack T. Harris Scholarship Fund
May 6, 1991.

...WHEREAS, Jack T. Harris, Sr. of Theodore,
Alabama, desires to establish a scholarship and award
to be available annually to "The Lyman Ward Military
Academy," Camp Hill, Alabama.

The award reference is to the Jack T. Harris, Sr. Award, presented annually to an academy cadet, "who demonstrates a desire to overcome obstacles and who exhibits perseverance and diligence to task."

The story just gets better and better and better. Where are you Ward and Carver? You must have known. You had to have known what was inside this boy in 1936. Through him, you live!

Harris to Lyman Ward Military Academy

December 1991 (handwritten)

…Count on this year after year. Also I will put $1,000 each year in the larger award as long as I can.

My regards, JTH

Jack Harris has come full circle with the academy; once an apprehensive interview candidate; then a determined student; and later, a grateful benefactor.

As he is determined to give back, he has fallen again – a serious fall this time.

Jack T. Harris

This story started with Jack sprawled on the floor in 1992, unable to move, bleeding and in pain. His life flashes before him. And now, he is back to present day.

He finds himself at the foot of a staircase. The blood from the injuries he sustained in the fall has dried and Jack finds that he is "still here." He begins to move. It's time for him to try once more – to get back up one more time.

In the manner of George W. Carver in his final years, Harris is resolute.

He struggles back to his feet; feeble and brave. As his letter to Lyman Ward Military Academy recalled,

---

"I'm still a tough old bird. I have never broke a bone falling, just cracked some...In June I messed up good. I am slowly getting back. My jaw is letting me chew and I can write a bit. ...Laying at the bottom of stairs over 2 hours bleeding, I thought all was over. I'm here anyway. ...October brings fond memories of the school when Dr. Ward had a cake at my plate and cake cut for everybody on October 26. I'll be 73 this time."

My best, JTH

"I'm still a tough old bird."

Harris to Lyman Ward Military
Academy
February 17, 1993 (handwritten)

...I'm behind on everything. I've messed
up this already. This past year has been
my worst yet – I don't even feel the pen
in my hand. No one can realize how all
this has hit me. So many falls and I'm
not as tough as I used to be – floor gets
harder every time. ...My greatest hope
always is that whatever I've done, I hope
others will do more and better. ...Add
check to other $6,000. Hope I can send
one each year.

Excuse writing, JTH

Harris to Lyman Ward Military
Academy
November 4, 1993 (handwritten)

...Check for award - $350. ...Having
trouble writing or anything.

JTH

Jacob T. Harris

"Having trouble writing or anything."

It was the "anything" that finally got him.

As many times as Jack got back up, as many times as he persisted, as many times as he stood tall for the youth of America, Father Time had his way with Jack. Jack T. Harris was seventy-five years old when he died in 1994.

The king of the roost joined Carver and Ward in the heavens above. Fate took, God gave. And what Jack had been given, he used every day of his life for the benefit of youth and the disabled – such as himself. He may have never considered himself disabled and he lived to serve others that they might feel the same. Giving back he did!!!

"I cannot think that in the last
analysis there is much of any
difference between the thing we
call death and that intangible
something, which we call growth."

Lyman Ward

"There would be no growth,
unless there was that change which
we call death. We are too finite...
to understand it all."

George Carver

XIII

Jack's Life Legacy: Giving Back

Dr. Carver bequeathed all he had to his beloved Tuskegee Institute.

His dear boy, Jack, must have inherited the generosity of spirit of his mentor; as in his twilight years, sixty years later, he decided to give everything back as well.

The scholarship endowment had been established as Jack's gift to the school that had molded his character. There would be more. To the organization that allowed him to mold the lives of other young people, he also left a legacy.

Upon his death, Jack T. Harris left a valuable piece of real estate on the waters of Mobile Bay to the Boys

& Girls Club of Greater Mobile and to Lyman Ward Military Academy; formerly The Southern Industrial Institute. He had purchased it for $1,600, in 1957, and it took him ten years to pay off the debt. Today, it is valued in seven figures.

Jack's gift gave his son and namesake the right to live his entire life on this beautiful property; and once he joined his father, the property would go to the school and the Boys & Girls Club.

As of this writing, Jack, Jr. was working with the Mobile Community Foundation to work out possible benefits that could accrue to his father's "two loves," in advance of the original plan.

Perhaps some of Sr.'s heart has been passed on to Jr.'s heart. Just as his father set up the Jack T. Harris Sr. Scholarship at Lyman Ward before his death, the son may be taking additional steps to honor his father. It is hoped that all of Jack Sr.'s important papers and memorabilia are being donated to the organization as well.

Jack answered his calling; he lived "Invictus," captaining his own soul to the end.

He fought for the opportunity to get into Lyman Ward's school, pulled his weight, endured grueling polio

Jack T. Harris

treatments, and doggedly propelled himself forward. He knew what he wanted and distilled his hopes into a simple sentence in his 1937 letter to Carver:

"*I want to make good in future life.*"

He grew to greatness, coping with and transcending his physical challenges, in order to conserve his energies for others. He listened to his inner voice, which urged him toward the non-profit sector and toward diverse young people who could blossom within his organization. He offered strength, shelter, and tenderness to others, just as he had received from his own role models.

His dedication drove him into the streets to try to stop fighting between youth gangs and he was violently assaulted on two separate occasions – yet pressed ahead.

Where did the equilibrium and single-mindedness come from? The influence of Carver and Ward undoubtedly contributed to the harmony in Jack's life. There was indeed a perceptible harmony in the rhythms of his life.

Harris seemed to result from, thrive on, and emanate harmony. Just as his mentors accepted, learned from, and valued differences, so did he. He embraced the nature of differences, and lived the spirit of Carver.

Glenn Clark quotes Carver in *The Man Who Talks with the Flowers*: "And God was not in the mountain, and not in the wind, not in the fire – but in the still, small voice…if we always listen to the still, small voice, all of life will unfold for us in harmony."

Jack listened to his still, small voice – a voice nurtured by Carver and Ward - a voice to be heard by thousands of youth.

Jack T. Harris

"Our days are numbered.
One of the primary goals in our lives
should be to prepare for our last day.
The legacy we leave is not just in our
possessions, but in the
quality of our lives."

Billy Graham

Jack's Family Legacy

XIV

A Father's Highest Achievement: A Son's Love

I thought all was over, that the story found its natural ending place with Jack's death. An emotional and educational odyssey was ending when my findings – the letters of Jack Harris and his star-crossed era neared completion in summer, 2004.

It had been nearly seventy years since Carver had steadfastly tried to infuse agility and strength into Jack's limbs, fifty years since Harris founded the Boys Club, and ten years since Jack had joined Carver and Ward in the heavens above.

It was only then – towards the end – that I actually went back again to where Jack had lived, walked the grounds where he'd walked, and visited where he'd worked. I wanted to breathe the air of confidence Jack had breathed. My friend, Dr. Mayberry always asked me, "When is enough, enough?". In this case, enough was not enough.

I needed to know more! I had to know more. Something was missing. Traveling back on I-65 to Mobile from Auburn, Alabama, I sought one final answer, one final concluding moment that celebrated the life and purpose of Jack, Sr. – something that said it far better than I might as the teller of this story.

Upon reaching Mobile, I met Jack's son. The meeting didn't produce the rest of the story; it was the whole story in microcosm.

On a hot, humid August day in Mobile, Jack Jr. was waiting outside his business for me. As I drove up, I thought of his father. I was nervous. He greeted me warmly and we went inside to cool off . It was the kind of day when the humidity made it feel equally uncomfortable inside and out, even with air conditioning.

Unsure if our meeting would be thirty minutes or three hours, I came prepared. Armed with letters, photos, a partial Manuscript, and a table of contents – I was ready.

Jack T. Harris

The meeting lasted nearly six hours. We started in Jack Jr.'s office, visited some of his father's friends and Scouts, stopped by Jack Jr.'s home, talked with his employees and friends, and ended up at the American Legion Lodge in Theodore, Alabama.

We began the day discussing Jack Sr.'s mother and step-father, Iva and Albert Hayes. "They were good folks and loved my father," the son explained. "I never knew of any time when my father was treated like he was disabled. To them, he was normal, as he was to me. My grandmother loved her son and my father always spoke of her privately with great admiration, great respect. She was a great southern lady.

"Pop's word was bankable and his tenacity to barrel through the tough times was unequaled. That was my pop."

As we talked, the son grew more animated, moving to the edge of his seat with pride. Every word about his father seemed to diminish the fifty-eight years of wrinkles I'd noticed when I first walked in. He'd recommend others for me to talk with and even picked up the phone to call them.

One call was to one of his father's best friends. Jack Jr. turned the phone over to me whispering, "This is Billy Fisher."

I grabbed the phone, introduced myself and said, "I understand Jack was your best friend."

Fisher responded, "Jack was my best friend, but I am not sure I was his. He had many best friends. He was a god to others and me. I thought the sun rose and set by Jack Harris. When I first met him, I was twelve years old and thought he was drunk because of his affliction. I knew what a drunk was because my parents owned three or four flophouses and I had seen many drunks.

"You could set your clock by Jack Harris. There was no better friend in life than Jack. I was with him when Jack Jr. was born and I was there when we laid him down ten years ago, in 1994. I literally spent much of my life being in service to Jack Harris; kind of his assistant in working with the youth of Mobile. I would not have wanted to spend my life any other way."

After the call, Jack Jr. continued, "I think of my father every day. I am so proud of what he accomplished in life. Funny, I do little things like him in some ways. My business card, for example, is green. Pop used to write in green ink so that people would remember the Boys Club.

"I think of my father every day."

"I never went two days in my life without seeing or talking with my father. We were buddies. There was

Jack T. Harris

just the two of us all my life. We had to make our way together. As I grew up, things Pop would say stuck with me that I will never forget. Part of what I remember was the way he treated people in his life.

"He treated all people the same all the time. That was one thing you could depend on with Pop. He learned that from Carver and Ward in his young life, as he told me so. It was in this way that my father made millions—in friendships.

"Pop headed up the Boy Scouts in Mobile for twenty-two years and then Troop 7 became part of the Boys Club that he founded in 1957. He started it with whites, then added blacks, then merged them together. That was what Pop always had in mind, that whites and blacks needed to be together. He had many black friends.

I wonder why?

"His measure of a person was always how the person thought of him or herself.

I wonder why?

"My father loved Dr. Carver. He respected him and considered Carver a friend, not just a mentor. Carver would introduce him to others at Tuskegee. I remember his telling me about being introduced to a great black businessman in Alabama, A. G. Gaston. Pop was impressed with Mr. Gaston. Gaston told him, 'Son, I got you from the time you are born to the time you die,' referring to his many businesses. My father never forgot that."

We drove to his father's land, the land Jack Sr. had spent $1,600 to acquire in 1957. It was a majestic eleven or so acres, overlooking the water. Tucked away near the rear of the property was a home. "My father and I built this house together, board by board," Jack Jr. shared. "Just the two of us. It was our project together in life. Just me and my Pop."

It was evident that the experience meant a great deal to the son. When he visits this hideaway on the water, he and his father are together again. It almost felt as if Jack Sr. was present there. *(Perhaps he was!)* His corner of the world on the water is the kind of place one's spirit never leaves.

Jack Jr. went inside, returned with a foldout presentation board, and suggested, "Let's go over to the American Legion Lodge and visit. I'd like to show you this."

At the Lodge, everyone in the place knew Jack Jr. When Charlie Beech approached us and learned I was writing a book about Jack Harris Sr., he said, "I was one of the Harris boys too. Jack Harris was one of the best men I ever knew."

After selecting a table, Jack Jr. unfolded the board. Lying in front of me was a presentation of the professional life

Jacob T. Harris

of Jack Harris, Sr. in the year 1977 – twenty years from the day the Boys Club was founded.

I flashed back to the teenaged Jack Harris writing to Carver that he wanted to make good with his life. Here I was, holding the "making good," some sixty-eight years later.

The title words were, "Professional Excellence."

Jack Jr.'s conversation pulled me back to the present. "Everywhere he went, I went. I turned the lights on ahead of my father in the cabins, in buildings. We were a team. Most people did not know that my father was blind in one eye also. But he saw more in one eye than most see with two. He walked with braces. But it never slowed him down.

"Everywhere he went, I went."

"With us, we worried about each other. There was no woman in the house, just us two. Today, when I shave, I see Pop in the mirror. I even use the same faces he used. I never wanted to be like him, as a boy growing up. Everybody kept telling me that I should grow up and be like my father, over and over, for years. Well, I rebelled. I knew they were right, but what did I know? Today, I would love to be like Pop.

"When I think about him, Pop didn't matter to Pop – what he did to help others is what mattered to Pop. You know, Pop and Coach Bear Bryant were friends. Coach Bryant would send kid teams down to Mobile, to play in a championship game with the Boys Club team. They worked that out together.

"He was the kind of man that great things always happened to because of the groundwork he laid. Educating people is what my Pop did, of any age. You can go into any business today in Mobile, and there is probably someone there who knew him. I am proud of that."

In this moment of the most intimate kind; a moment that only God would orchestrate, I looked into the son's eyes. Deep within was Jack, Sr. – my dear boy, Jack. All those letters, all those hot peanut oil treatments, all those falls and getting back up again.

The silence was perfect. This was it. The son talked with peace, pride, and love about his father. As he spoke, I asked what he would say to his dad if he had one more visit with him.

"If I had my father back and he was right here with me, just the two of us, I would tell him, 'Pop, I love you.'

In tears, it was uttered one more time.

"Pop, I love you."

Jack T. Harris

This legacy of Jack Harris, Sr. must surely rank as his most meaningful; enduring filial respect and affection – magnificent memories in the voice and eyes of a loving son.

I am reminded of my own father. He died an early death and I was much too young to appreciate all that he was to me. There is a quote he loved and it seems fitting to apply it to the end of our journey with Jack Harris. It was written on my father's high school graduation announcement from Waterbury High School in Vermont – Class of 1936. It reads, "Nunc deducimus, ubi stabimus?" – Now we launch, where shall we anchor?

Jack Jr. anchored with – Pop. I love you.
As a story, My dear boy, Jack shall anchor here!

"Nunc deducimus, ubi stabimus?"

"My father willed his estate to two wonderfully important organizations for the development of youth. I have never questioned that decision, but I would be less than honest if I told that it would not have helped me. Far more important, though, he left me something I treasure daily - right here." (Pointing to his heart)

Jack Harris, Jr.

Letters to Remember
Jack By

Camp Hill, Alabama
February 8, 1938

Dear Dr Carver,

I am very sorry
that I haven't written
lately but my work
here had been taking
all of my time.

Dr Ward is always
asking if I have written
you. I think about you
and what you have done
for me often. My room
mate and I talk of you
while he rubs me
with the oil. He rubs
me three nights a week
before bed time. I
stretch out on the bed
and he does a good job
on me.

You remember Mr
Scott who went with
me to see you at the
hospital? He has left
us to take a position
with the government.
We hated very much
to loose him. I had a
letter from Mr Scott
their week and he said
tell you I enjoyed very
much meeting you
and wishes we could
have visited longer.

When Mr Scott left I was put in charge of the dormitory until another one could be contacted. I have been very busy helping him.

Dr Carver I am playing basketball. I enjoy the exercise and I believe it helps me.

I am very anxious to get over to see you. I would like you to get me over and have improved by doing as you tell me.

I saw in the paper that you were back at work and it made me feel very good to know you were back. I am very interested in your health and want you to take care of yourself.

If there are any things you think not please let me know.

Very truly yours
Jacob T. Harris

Camp Hill, Ala.
Oct 31, 1931

Dear Dr Carver,

I am sorry I haven't written in quite a while. My studies are very hard this year and I put all my time on them.

Hope you had a nice summer traveling. Sorry I could not see you for treatment.

School has been going strong and I am very proud to be able to be here. Dr Ward is very nice and always asking of you.

My school work is good. I was one of the twelve students to make above 90 on the studies. We were on the stage.

Everyone says I am improving ever so much. They think it is like that I play football. I still use the oil but not like I should I guess. The lights go out before I finish rubbing. I get I have got it in red.

I wish you would please give me an idea about the oil. Shall I use it the same as you said. I just use it at bedtimes. Where should I rub, etc.

The first chance I get I will come over to see you.

Yours very truly
Jack T. Harris

AFTERWORD

Tracey Elofson, Her God and Disability

As I've come to know those with a disability – visible or invisible – I've learned that they possess remarkable degrees of hope, resilience, and sensitivity.

They see things invisible to many of us.

They wait hopefully and patiently, knowing any accomplishment requires small, difficult steps.

Although some can't put one foot in front of the other, they walk this earth with a distinctive, enviable harmony. A closer understanding and appreciation by all Americans of the lives, abilities, and goals of the disabled can only lead to a more enriched society.

The facts are sobering.

According to past data from the National Center for Health Statistics, the U.S. has 32.6 million non-institutionalized people, whose usual activities are limited, due to chronic conditions. This represents 11.9 percent of the population. Among adults, 7 million (3.4%) have trouble hearing, 20.4 million (10%) have difficulty with vision, 12.9 million (6.5%) cannot walk a quarter-mile, 25.2 million (12.4%) have moderate mobility difficulty, and 20.4 million (10.0%) experience severe mobility difficulty. There are 6.2 million people aged sixty-five years and older who need help with personal care. Among children ages three-seventeen, 4.7 million (7.7%) have been diagnosed with learning disabilities.

One measure of America's greatness and goodness is its concern for those who are afflicted. Our collective desire to bolster the lives of the disabled is evident in research programs, volunteerism, non-profits, and a determination to offer mobility and access to all.

Coming to grips with treatment of the afflicted has proven a learning curve for the country, over time. The fact is, though, we all belong to circles of affliction and we persevere through our own adversity. In our relationships of difference, we all ask the same thing; the dignity and understanding that lead to self worth.

Jack T. Harris

That's what the story of Jack Harris, his family, and his mentors is about; the shared human condition and the respect, love, and meaning we all crave.

Disability is everywhere. The stigma associated with it is running rampant.

We notice it more as our individual circles of affliction blossom. As I inventoried those I know well, who have afflictions, I count thirteen in my life who have some form of disability, and I do not believe I am alone in this respect.

We all learn differently.

For me, there has been no greater teacher and leader about disability than my sister, Tracey Warren Elofson. She is stricken with ALS.

Tracey represents millions who live with affliction. It is they who best understand their captivity and choose to turn it to the best possible account.

The afflicted seem to understand that fretting over that from which they have been removed, or which has been taken away, will not make things better. The bond is only tightened by our stretching it to the uttermost. The impatient horse, which will not quietly endure his halter, only strangles himself in his stall.

Jack understood.

Tracey understands. She appears to know something we unafflicted do not and it is something that cannot be explained.

But just because we do not experience what she does, does not mean that we cannot work at better understanding.

I believe she sees life better, more clearly. She understands patience and waiting far better. She lives with a consciousness that the hopeful unknown is close behind the visible scene of things.

Anyone who loves another with a crippling and life-taking illness knows what I'm saying. – Bucky Elofson and his and Tracey's four girls (Hope, Ashlyn, Megan, and Kathleen) have become angels in every possible way – and more than I ever thought possible.

During the week of June 29, 2013, Tracey and I had a three p.m. date of sorts, every day. I would read to her. It took five days – some five hours, to finish the book. After we finished, her response (in writing, as she could not speak) was one word – "Profound." The book? *My Dear Boy, Jack*. I knew then that this "wine" was ready for others to consume.

Thank you Tracey, for sacrificing all you are in the name of His love. May we all quietly endure our halters. If I were looking into your eyes just now, I would say - I love you Tracey, with all a brotherly love can give!!

Jack T. Harris

"I do love humanity, and why shouldn't
I? When humanity has been so kind
and gracious to me. If it hadn't been
for this affliction (polio), I would have
never met the lovely people that I
have, and who have contributed so
much to my happiness. Think what
I would have missed in life."

George W. Carver

"In that temple of learning whither he
has gone I am sure that his valor will
bring fresh luster to its renown."

Lyman Ward

IN APPRECIATION

Extraordinary Approval, Support, Cooperation, and Dealing with the Untimely Deaths of Dear Mentors

The cooperation from others was extraordinary.

The learning curve for yours truly was beyond words. At my side was the greatest team one could ever assemble. And then, one by one, they passed away:

Ellen Piazza, (July 10, 2007). Editor of
My Dear Boy, Jack

Dr. B. D. Mayberry (February 8, 2009). Friend and Mentor

Virginia Hicks (June 22, 2010). Book Critic

Kathryn Tucker Windham (June 12, 2011). Storyteller and Friend

Harold Hicks (February 6, 2012). Book Critic

Paul Davis (September 23, 2012). Friend and Journalist – Newspaper Publisher

One death might have stopped this work. But six? It was shut down – until now.

The first six months of 2013 produced a renewed spirit to complete what was started. Sister Tracey had something to do with the restart!!!

Sincere thanks to: Tuskegee University Archives (Dr. Benjamin Payton, Cynthia Wilson), Lyman Ward Military Academy (formerly The Southern Industrial Institute – (Albert Hovey, and Maj. Gen. Clyde Hennies), The Lyman C. Ward Family (Ms. Mary Bernard, granddaughter of Ward), The Jack T. Harris Family (Jack Jr., Cullen, and Albert), the Boys and Girls Clubs of South Alabama (Mary Zoghby), The Library of Congress (Dr. Barbara Kraft), Ms. Margaret Washington Clifford (granddaughter of Booker T. Washington), The University of Southern Mississippi Archives,

Jack T. Harris

St. Lawrence University Archives and Rockefeller University Archives.

Few things in life are as rewarding as telling a story about another's journey through life. In some instances, there were moments when I felt as though the story warranted more of an author's will. However, it was more often the case that just the opposite was true. This work animated itself through the life lived by Jack Harris. It depended upon my getting the raw material and good quotes and then using them effectively. In many instances, I needed to step aside. It is an overstatement to say that I wrote this story, for it was more like the managing of a process.

I have learned much – about affliction and overcoming adversity, the importance of effective mentoring, and the extreme value of letter writing. The assistance of twenty-plus people and/or their institutions over three years, to ensure that Jack Harris will never be forgotten has been truly amazing.

Dr. B. D. Mayberry gave me the staying power to see this work through when times were tough. It was important to stay close to Carver's spirit and Mayberry always helped me do that.

Ellen Piazza's editing helped me to shape and structure the manuscript; to give it a conversational rhythm and needed tightness. When she first received the manuscript, it was in excess of 42,000 words and at printing is 30,736. Her knife was sharp and at first, it hurt. However, we worked vigorously to maintain the integrity of the story. Without Ms. Piazza and Dr. Mayberry, there would be no story to share.

I shall always appreciate the many who worked to tell the story of Jack Harris, a little boy in 1935; in *My Dear Boy, Jack.*

The loss of three advance readers of the work was a major upset in the plan, as their delight in the reading showed me that the story has an important message and is worthy of publishing.

As the months of working on this book turned into years, I became forever grateful to those who took the time to teach. Only now do I understand how ill equipped I was in the beginning, for I have finally learned that the best stories tell themselves.

And yet, it took one more person to launch this work.

Three years ago, I met Mark Victor Hansen at a leadership roundtable. He was formally introduced to me by our mutual friend, Mo Siegel. Mo asked me if I knew who Mark was and my answer was no, aside from what was indicated on his nametag. "He is the co-founder of the *Chicken Soup for the Soul* book series," Mo informed me. "Five hundred-million books sold."

Jack T. Harris

Mark and I met several times during those four days, which included my giving him this and another leadership manuscript. After reading them, he said, "I want to help you with this leadership work." Three years later, Mark has provided meaningful leadership, introductions, and counsel to the upcoming *Leadership for the Soul* series of books, with Volume I being – *My Dear Boy, Jack.*

> **"I want to help you with this**
> **leadership work."**

He did and then - I did!

Upon Mark's counsel, FriesenPress came into my life, and off we go to publishing Leadership for the Soul Series - starting with My Dear Boy, Jack.

At the very center of this unfolding journey, there has been one person who understands so much and loves so deep.

"Adversity will finally turn out to be the advantage of the right if we are only willing to keep on working and to wait patiently. There are harvests, which can grow only after the plowshare has done its work. Out of suffering have emerged the strongest souls; the most massive characters are seamed with scars; martyrs have put on their coronation robes glittering with fire, and through their tears have the sorrowful first seen the gates of heaven."

Chapin

CROSSING THE FINISH LINE AT LAST

The Wind Beneath My Wings – Char Warren

Char knew. Char believed in me. She knew the truth of this story and its message. At every departure for Tuskegee, Vail, and the world, her love became the wind beneath my wings. She put up with so much and more so, encouraged me onward and upward. She saw my joy when I found my grandfather in the George W. Carver papers – a letter to him and one back from him. We have cried together and we have laughed at much during this process of managing the letters and the many messages they deliver. Please know, my dear Char, that what has been made possible here would never have been at all, if you did not believe that this would one day come together for the good of the human condition. Char has been to me what Ward and Carver were to my dear boy, Jack. In 2013, as my sister has been dealing with ALS, it brought this book back off the shelf to finish it. The finish line has been reached and crossed – and I am still standing. Thank you Char. I love you for all that you are, by standing in for all I am not! With each "I love you" said to her, her immediate response is always, "I love you more!"

"I love you more!"

27:17

Jacob T. Harris

Works Cited:

Seavey, Nina, Wagner, Paul and Smith, Jane, *A Paralyzing Fear: The Triumph Over Polio in America*, New York, TV Books LLC, 1998, Print

Clark, Glenn, *The Man Who Talks with the Flowers: The Life Story of George Washington Carver*, Austin, MN, Macalster Park Pub. Co, 1976, Print

The President's Birthday Magazine, National Foundation for Infantile Paralysis, Jan. 30, 1938, Print

Collier, Peter and Horowitz, David, *The Fords: An American Epic*, San Francisco, Encounter Books, 1987, Print

As iron sharpens iron,

so one person

sharpens another.

Proverbs: 27:17

ABOUT THE AUTHOR

Toby Warren is the founder of the National Leadership Congress – a servant leadership institution dedicated to advocacy, education, research, and training for veterans, families, communities, and businesses, with special emphasis on trauma, PTSD and suicide prevention. After discovering 1930s letters from a polio-afflicted little boy to George Washington Carver, he was deeply impacted by them. The strength, courage and triumph over disability they demonstrated influenced him to share the story. Warren has also published *Where Will We Be When We Get Where We're Going? – A General's Spiritual Journey,* and *A Tender Warrior.* Warren and his wife, Char, reside in Auburn, Al.